Finding the Lost Cities

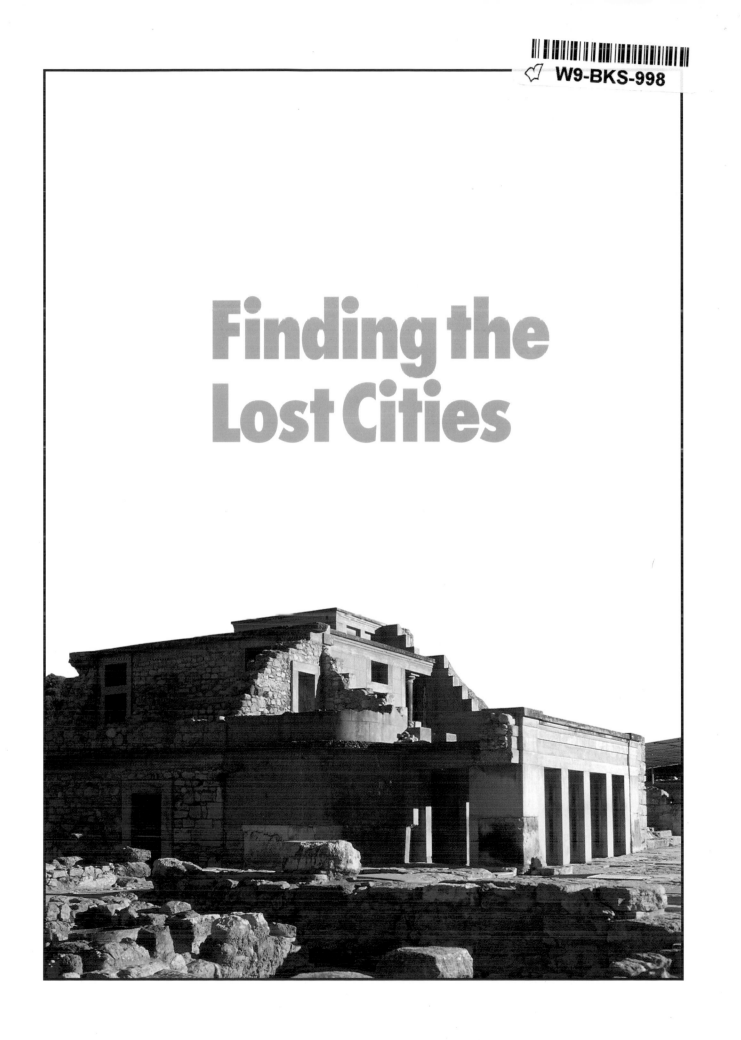

Finding the Lost Cities

Rebecca Stefoff

Oxford University Press • *New York*

To my father, with love

Oxford University Press

Oxford   New York
Athens   Auckland   Bangkok   Bogotá   Bombay
Buenos Aires   Calcutta   Cape Town   Dar es Salaam   Delhi
Florence   Hong Kong   Istanbul   Karachi
Kuala Lumpur   Madras   Madrid   Melbourne
Mexico City   Nairobi   Paris   Singapore
Taipei   Tokyo   Toronto
and associated companies in
Berlin   Ibadan

Design: Loraine Machlin
Picture research: Patricia Burns

Library of Congress Cataloging-in-Publication Data
Stefoff, Rebecca.
Finding the Lost Cities / by Rebecca Stefoff
  p.   cm.
Includes bibliographical references and index.
1. Extinct cities—Juvenile literature. 2. Cities and towns, Ancient—Juvenile
literature. 3. Civilization, Ancient—Juvenile literature. [1. Extinct cities.
2. Cities and towns, Ancient. 3. Civilization, Ancient. 4. Archaeology.]
I. Title.
CC176.S74   1997
930.1—dc20   96-9802
                CIP

ISBN 0-19-509249-X

9 8 7 6 5 4 3 2 1

Printed in Hong Kong
on acid-free paper

On the cover: A building carved into the rock walls at Petra (World Monuments Fund). *Inset:* Leonard Woolley removes a buried figurine from the ground at Ur (© British Museum).
Half title: One of the structures discovered and restored by Arthur Evans at Knossos.
Frontispiece: The ruins of Angkor Wat.

Contents

Introduction
From the Sands of Time

As the sun sank below the western cliffs, the last golden shafts of sunlight fanned out across the Valley of the Kings. It was late in the afternoon of November 26, 1922. Howard Carter did not see the sunlight. He was standing at the end of a 27-foot-long rock-walled tunnel at the bottom of a flight of 16 steps that had been cut into this valley floor by stonemasons more than 3,000 years earlier. In front of him was a sealed doorway that bore the ancient royal emblems of the Egyptian pharaohs. It also showed signs of having been opened and resealed.

Carter hoped that beyond the door lay the tomb of Tutankhamen, the young pharaoh who had ruled Egypt for a decade until his death around 1325 B.C. He feared, however, that the tomb had been looted, either in ancient times or in the recent past. Perhaps he would find only an empty chamber.

Howard Carter was an archaeologist, someone who studies human history by examining the relics of earlier cultures. He had been fascinated by ancient Egypt for more than 30 years. For 15 of

The golden mask of King Tutankhamen lay buried for more than 30 centuries in Egypt's Valley of the Kings (background), until Howard Carter discovered and entered his tomb in 1922.

those years, he had been seeking Tutankhamen's tomb. For the past six years, his search for the tomb had been funded by Lord Carnarvon, a wealthy Englishman who shared Carter's dream of finding the boy-king's final resting place. But Carnarvon had grown discouraged. He had told Carter that this was the last season of digging he would support.

Carter's hands trembled as he picked up a hammer and chisel. Behind him in the narrow stone tunnel stood Carnarvon, his daughter, and Carter's assistant. They waited in silence while Carter chipped a small hole through the plaster-and-stone door. He held up a candle and looked through the hole. "As my eyes grew accustomed to the light," Carter later wrote, "details of the room within emerged slowly from the mist, strange animals, statues, and gold—everywhere the glint of gold."

The archaeologist was unable to speak. "Can you see anything?" Lord Carnarvon asked anxiously. "Yes, wonderful things," Carter answered, like a man lost in a dream. Howard Carter had found the tomb of the pharaoh Tutankhamen, untouched for thousands of years.

Carter had made one of the most sensational discoveries in the history of archaeology. His dogged refusal to abandon the search for Tutankhamen's tomb, the romantic story of the boy-king who came to the throne at 9 and died at 19, and above all the splendid richness and beauty of the 5,000 items recovered from the tomb made "King Tut's Treasure" one of the best known of all archaeological finds. Carter's 1922 discovery also marked the end of an era: the heroic age of archaeology.

That heroic age began in 1798, when Napoléon Bonaparte tried to conquer Egypt for France. His army was accompanied by a corps of scholars and scientists, to whom Napoléon gave the task of measuring, sketching, and studying the monuments of ancient Egypt, which were then little known to the outside world. Although Napoleon's military invasion ended in a humiliating defeat by the British navy, the invasion of the scientists brought lasting results. The many books and illustrations they published upon returning to France awakened a passionate interest in the ancient world among Europeans and Americans.

Howard Carter (left) prepares to remove one of two life-size figures of the young king found in his tomb. Compartments under the king's kilt, perhaps meant to hold sacred religious documents, were empty when Carter discovered the tomb.

Awed by the relics of Egypt's ancient glory, soldiers and scholars from Napoléon Bonaparte's French army clambered over the Sphinx and the Pyramids, drawing pictures and taking measurements.

In the decades that followed, explorers, scholars, and adventurers spread out across the globe. Some studied ancient relics that had been known for centuries, such as the monuments of Rome, the temples of Greece, and the Pyramids and Sphinx of Egypt. Others searched for new windows into the distant past, evidence of ancient civilizations that had been buried and forgotten for centuries. Some of these searchers discovered lost cities. These discoveries were greeted with rapturous excitement by the public; in the 19th century, as today, the finding of a lost city was front-page news. Yet these exciting discoveries did more than arouse public interest in lost civilizations. Each find added something to our knowledge of the past, and each represented a new stage in the development of archaeology as a scientific discipline.

The 12 lost cities described in this book span the globe, from Africa, the Mediterranean, and the Middle East to Southeast Asia and the Americas. They are presented in the order of their discovery or rediscovery by the modern world. The last of these discoveries was made by Leonard Woolley in Iraq in 1922—the

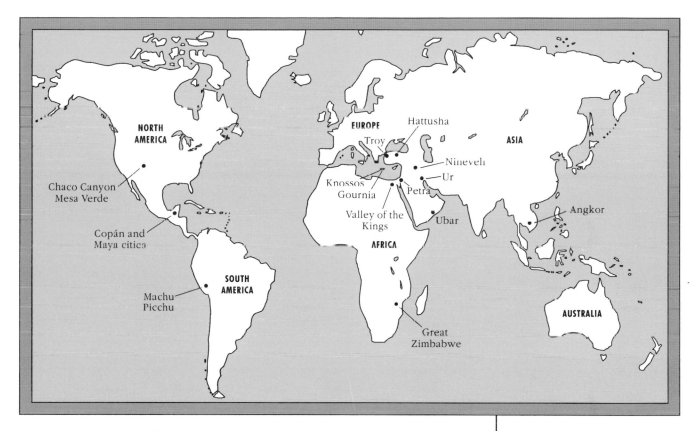

The lost cities in this book are located on five continents.

same year that Howard Carter made his sensational discovery in the Valley of the Kings. By that time archaeology was becoming a well-organized, modern science involving teamwork, planning, and technology. The age of the lone adventurer had ended. The age of the scientific explorer, however, continues to this day.

Lost cities have always fascinated us. Archaeology has shown us that for thousands of years people have come together in cities to live, work, raise families, worship, govern, and trade. The city is the emblem of civilization, with all its blessings and discontents, and by studying the cities that people have left behind, we look across the centuries into their hearts and minds. Said Marcus Terentius Varro, a Roman scholar of the 1st century B.C., "It was divine nature which gave us the country, and man's skill that built the cities."

CHAPTER 1

Petra
On Forbidden Ground

*I*n 1812, the lands at the eastern end of the Mediterranean Sea were part of the Ottoman Empire, a Muslim state centered in Turkey. After centuries of warfare with Christian Europe, the Ottoman Turks—and their subjects throughout the Middle East and North Africa—regarded Europeans with suspicion. A Christian traveling through Muslim lands was likely to be treated as a spy and either expelled or killed.

Sheikh Ibrahim ibn Abdullah, a traveling merchant, aroused no such suspicion. Full-bearded, dressed in a Turkish turban and robe, he spoke Arabic fluently and observed all the rituals of Islam, the Muslim faith. Such was his learning that the people he met on his travels through the Muslim world accepted him as an expert on Islamic law. They would have been astounded to learn that his real name was Johann Ludwig Burckhardt.

Burckhardt was born in 1784 in Switzerland and educated in Germany and England, where he studied Arabic. In 1809, he was hired by the British African Association to investigate one of the geographic mysteries of the age: Were

A mosaic figure representing springtime decorated the floor of a church built in the 6th century in Petra. The tombs carved into the wall (background) are 400 years older.

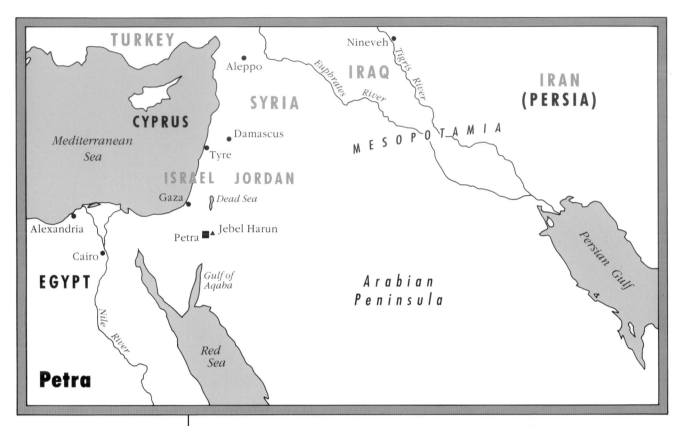

the two great rivers of North Africa, the Niger and the Nile, really the same river? Some geographers thought that the two rivers flowed from a common source or were joined somewhere in the vast desert interior of North Africa, a region that Europeans had only begun to explore. Other geographers maintained—correctly, as it was later determined—that the two rivers were entirely separate.

The British African Association asked Burckhardt to settle the question of a link between the Niger and the Nile through firsthand exploration. Burckhardt accepted the challenge. His first step, he decided, would be to go to Syria and spend several years perfecting his Arabic. Then he would move on to Cairo, Egypt, where he could join a caravan across the Sahara Desert to the Niger area. Burckhardt grew a beard, transformed himself into Sheikh Ibrahim ibn Abdullah, and set out for Aleppo, Syria.

Burckhardt did more than study the Muslim world—he came to be at home in it and developed a deep respect for Muslim culture. He also possessed an unquenchable geographic curiosity, which led him down many side roads on the way to carrying out his appointed task. One such road led him to a city that few Europeans—perhaps none—had seen since the 12th century.

Petra was not exactly a *lost* city. Its existence was well remembered by historians. In the great days of the Roman Empire, the second and third centuries A.D., Petra had been one of the leading cities of Rome's eastern provinces. Yet Petra had fallen into a long decline, and by Burckhardt's time it was seldom visited except by the local Bedouin, nomadic Arab desert dwellers. As far as the outside world was concerned, Petra's location—hidden in a gorge between the Dead Sea and the Gulf of 'Aqaba, in what is now the country of Jordan—was a matter of considerable mystery. In 1806, a German scholar named Ulrich Seetzen, traveling through Ottoman lands in Arab disguise, had heard a Bedouin mention "the ruins of Petra." Seetzen tried to sneak into Petra, but when he was found to be a Christian in disguise he was killed.

Six years later, on his way south from Syria to Cairo, Burckhardt found himself in the vicinity of Petra and decided to see this long-forgotten city. His disguise was better than Seetzen's, or perhaps he was simply luckier, for he reached the city unharmed. The approach to Petra, he discovered, was a narrow gorge, 200 feet deep, called the Siq. This natural passageway snaked into the center of a rocky fastness on the slope of a mountain called Jabal Harun (mentioned in the Bible as Mount Hor). Rounding the last turn of the dark, echoing Siq, the traveler was confronted with one of the most dramatic sights in the world: the front of a building 100 feet wide and 130 feet high, ornamented with towering columns and larger-than-life statues, all carved out of the solid rock wall of the gorge. This building was called the Khazneh. The most extraordinary feature of the Khazneh was its color. The building was carved into a sandstone wall that glowed, when the sun shone on it, in vivid shades of pink, red, orange, and crimson, streaked with bands of yellow, white, and purple.

Beyond the Khazneh, the Siq opened into a broad canyon about a mile across. This canyon was a city buried inside a mountain, surrounded by steep natural rock walls that were broken in only two

Johann Ludwig Burckhardt, disguised as Sheikh Ibrahim, in a sketch made in Cairo in 1817.

No army could take Petra by storm. This deep gorge, called the Siq, is one of only two narrow passageways into the city, which lies hidden in a canyon walled by rugged mountainsides.

places, where narrow gorges offered routes in or out of the valley. All around were more structures cut into the rock. Some of them were little more than simple square chambers, almost caves. Others were large and elaborate, with stairways and statues, grand doorways and multistoried pillared fronts, all carved into the red and pink rock face. These structures were the tombs and temples of a bygone people called the Nabataeans.

The Nabataeans were Arabian nomads who, in about the 6th century B.C., migrated north from the Arabian Peninsula into the region that is now Jordan and southern Syria. They built many settlements, but chief among these was Petra, their capital. The site of Petra had much to recommend it. For one thing, it was easy to defend. No army could muster a mass attack against Petra, for the only access was through the narrow gorges. Second, the highland plateau around the city had forests for timber and grassland for grazing. Third, a spring provided a reliable, year-round water source.

By the 4th century B.C., the Nabataeans were taking full advantage of yet another feature of the site: Petra lay near the major caravan route linking Asia and Arabia to Europe. Traders with their heavily loaded camels carried goods from all over the ancient world past Petra's doorstep. Incense from Arabia, spices from India by way of the Persian Gulf, gold from Egypt, and silks from China all passed through Petra on their way to the marketplaces of Damascus, Tyre, and Gaza, which in turn were gateways to Greece and other Mediterranean destinations. The Nabataeans profited from Petra's closeness to the trade route—sometimes by simple piracy, but mostly by charging taxes and fees on the commerce that passed through their territory. The people of Petra also hired themselves out as guides through the region and provided food and water—for a fee—to travelers and their caravan animals.

Petra had become the Nabataean capital by the 3rd century B.C. The practice of excavating tombs in the rock walls was already well established; some archaeologists think that it may have been begun by earlier peoples who lived in the area and were displaced or absorbed by the Nabataeans. Although little is known of the religion of the Nabataeans, scholars believe that they may have regarded their dead kings as gods. The tombs of these god-kings functioned as temples. The Nabataeans built other temples as well. Some were carved into the rock, but the largest was a freestanding structure built in the 1st century B.C. It may have been dedicated to Dusares, the chief god of Petra, whose symbol was a block of stone.

The Nabataeans reached the height of their prosperity and importance after the 2nd century B.C. At its greatest extent, their kingdom stretched from Damascus to the Red Sea. But in one way especially their influence spread even beyond the borders of their kingdom and was longer-lasting: The Nabataeans' writing evolved into the modern Arabic script, which is used today across a large part of the world. Under their king Aretas III, who ruled from 80 to 65 B.C., the Nabataeans minted their own coins and built a Greek-style amphitheater. Petra grew famous throughout the ancient world. Wherever camel caravans linked communities with the bonds of trade, even as far away as China, people had heard about the fabulous city in the rock.

During the 1st century A.D., the Romans took control of territory around Petra. In 106, Rome acquired Petra itself. The city and the region around it became a province of the Roman Empire known as Arabia Petraea. It was one of the empire's most prosperous provinces—in some years it produced as much as a quarter of the economic output of the entire Roman Empire.

For a time Petra flourished under Roman rule. Roman engineers paved the caravan route and improved Petra's irrigation system. But trade, the backbone of Petra's economy, was beginning to change. More goods were being carried by sea; Alexandria, an Egyptian city on the Mediterranean coast, was taking some business away from Petra. The land routes were changing, too. North of Petra the Romans built a road connecting Damascus, in Syria, with Mesopotamia (present-day Iraq). This road drew even more traffic away from Petra. By the 3rd century, Petra's wealth and power had diminished greatly. In the 4th century, Petra became part of the Byzantine, or Eastern Roman, Empire. During this period it was a Christian city, the seat of an archbishop of the Byzantine, or Eastern Orthodox, Church. In the 7th century, Islam arose in Arabia and swiftly spread across much of western Asia and North Africa. Arabia Petraea became a minor province in an Islamic empire that would eventually stretch from Spain to Afghanistan.

By that time, however, Petra was all but abandoned. The rock-walled city rose to prominence again a few centuries later during the Crusades, the series of struggles between the Islamic powers and the Christian nations of Europe for control of the Near East. When the European Crusaders established a short-lived kingdom in the region, Petra became one of their strongholds. They held Petra until 1189; the ruins of their castle still stand amid the earlier relics of Petra's Nabataean glory. After the 12th century Petra was once again abandoned, except for the Bedouin and herdspeople who continued to use the tombs as shelters, and it was forgotten by the West until Burckhardt's visit.

For Burckhardt, Petra was simply one of many remarkable sights encountered during his travels. He went on to Cairo, traveled south on the Nile toward Ethiopia, and then crossed the Red Sea to Arabia, eventually returning to Cairo. In letters to the British African Association, he explained that he was waiting for an opportunity to join a caravan into the western desert, and that as soon as he could do so he would proceed to carry out his original mission, the exploration of the Niger River. Unfortunately, Burckhardt fell ill and died in Cairo in 1817 without ever getting near the Niger. But he had taken reams of notes during the course of his wanderings through Syria, Arabia, and the Nile Valley, and these the Association published in five thick volumes between 1819 and 1831.

One of Burckhardt's volumes, *Travels in Syria and the Holy Land* (1822), contained a description of Petra that aroused much excitement in Europe. A

trickle of adventurous Europeans began braving the hazards of the journey to see Petra—where they established a tradition of writing their names on the wall of the Khazneh. In 1830 a French traveler named Leon de Laborde published an account of his journey to Petra that was illustrated with magnificent drawings of the rock-cut tombs and temples. In 1835, this volume came into the hands of John Lloyd Stephens, a 30-year-old American tourist who was browsing through a bookstall in Paris. Suddenly, Stephens was filled with the desire to see long-lost Petra for himself. He went first to Egypt, where he examined the temples of Luxor and other antiquities from the age of the pharaohs. Then, costumed as a

Petra is filled with the crumbling remains of earlier civilizations, from the Nabataeans of the 6th century B.C. to the Christian Crusaders of the 12th century A.D.

The Romans built this theater when Petra was one of Rome's most prized possessions. After Roman power faded, the city belonged to the Christian Byzantine empire and then to the Islamic empire that arose in the 7th century.

merchant from Cairo, accompanied by an Italian servant who also wore Arab garb, he made his way to Petra, paying a considerable sum in bribes to the local Bedouin chieftain.

Like Burckhardt, Stephens was stunned by the sudden beauty of the Khazneh, which he called "a temple, delicate and limpid, carved like a cameo from a solid mountain wall." He proudly added "the name of an American citizen" to the tiny roster of tourists' names on the wall and proceeded to explore the tombs and monuments. They had long ago been stripped of everything of value. Now they were filled with dung from the nomads' animals and blackened with the smoke of their fires.

Stephens sat in the huge amphitheater carved out of solid rock and gazed out at the canyon, trying to do justice to the glorious colors of the rock city as he wrote in his journal. He was surprised by how well-preserved most of the ruins were; later he wrote, "The whole theater is in such a state of preservation, that if the tenants of the tombs around could once more rise into life, they might take their old places in the seats." This was the sort of sensation that 19th-century European and American travelers loved: Citizens of modern nations, caught up in the progress brought on by the Industrial Revolution, they thrilled to the poignant sight of ruins, the impressive relics of bygone grandeur, half-lost in some remote and forbidding landscape. The English poet Percy Bysshe Shelley had evoked this feeling in his 1817 poem "Ozymandias," which describes the giant statue of an ancient king, now lying shattered amid "the lone and level sands."

Stephens evoked it, too, in a book called *Incidents of Travel in Arabia Petraea* (1837), which he published upon returning to New York.

Stephens's book was reviewed by American poet and critic Edgar Allan Poe, who praised it highly. *Incidents of Travel in Arabia Petraea* became a best-seller in the United States and England. It helped to keep interest in Petra alive, and it inspired the poem "Petra" (1845) by John William Burgon, who would be utterly forgotten today but for these two haunting and often-quoted lines:

> Match me such a marvel save in Eastern clime,
> A rose-red city half as old as time.

More recently, Petra was immortalized in a different art form when filmmakers Steven Spielberg and George Lucas filmed the final scenes of their movie *Indiana Jones and the Last Crusade* there.

In the 19th century, curious travelers continued to make their way to Petra. Among them were the archaeologists Heinrich Schliemann, who later discovered Troy, and Austen Henry Layard, who later excavated the Mesopotamian city of Nineveh. But the opposition of the local Bedouin and the turbulent political situation of the whole region prevented serious, sustained archaeological work at the site. When World War I (1914–18) spread to the Middle East, Petra served as a strategic hideout for Arab guerrillas led by British soldier T. E. Lawrence, who entered history as "Lawrence of Arabia." Lawrence and his followers lived for a short time in some of the 500 or so caves that the ancient Nabataeans had carved into the valley walls.

Petra became a tourist attraction in the 20th century. At the same time, it became the subject of serious archaeological study. Since the early years of the century, German, British, Jordanian, Swiss, and American archaeologists have surveyed and excavated at Petra. Their work has led to a new and deeper understanding of the city's place in the ancient world. To early explorers like Burckhardt and Stephens, Petra was interesting chiefly because of its connection with ancient Rome. But historians now realize that Petra was the center of an important civilization—the Nabataean civilization—centuries before Rome became a power in the Middle East.

Lawrence of Arabia, as British soldier T. E. Lawrence came to be called, used Petra's caves as a hideout during World War I.

The first modern archaeological expeditions to Petra surveyed the rock-cut tombs and temples. Researchers established that Petra's architecture incorporates elements of style from Egypt, Syria, Mesopotamia, Greece, and Rome, as might be expected in a crossroads city. Some important recent work at Petra, however, goes beyond the famed rock-cut monuments to reveal new facets of this ancient city.

Much of the attention given to Petra over the years has focused on the tombs. As a result, people often think of Petra as a necropolis, a city of the dead. Archaeologists today, on the other hand, are increasingly interested in how Petra's people lived. They are tracing the Nabataean caravan tracks that were later overlaid with Roman roads, and they are excavating the three large marketplaces that were once crowded with merchants' stalls and with the stamping, milling horses and camels of the caravans. Archaeologists are also studying the water-storage system developed by the Nabataeans. This system included a large cistern or reservoir carved in the rock to store water from the spring and from rainfall, with an aqueduct that carried water into a smaller reservoir in the heart of the city. The Nabataeans also ran lines of clay pipes directly from the spring to various parts of the city. The Romans, skilled builders of aqueducts, improved the Nabataean water-supply system after Petra became a Roman province.

Another recent discovery has shown that the Nabataeans were not simply traders; they also manufactured excellent pottery, which they exported. Their earthenware was thin and delicate, decorated with images from nature, such as branches and leaves. Because Petra was a center of wealth, it attracted artists and scholars from all over the Nabataean realm. Their masterpieces may still be waiting to be discovered in Petra's buried ruins.

Scholars now estimate that as many as 30,000 people lived in Petra during its heyday. The city was much larger than the earliest European visitors suspected. The majority of its structures were not carved out of the rock walls, but were freestanding buildings that fell into ruin and were covered with windblown sand as the years passed. Most of Petra, in fact, remains unexcavated, and many of its mysteries are still unsolved. In 1994, an archaeologist working at the site said, "Most of the city structures have been covered by naturally deposited sand. The winds in this area are very strong, so I expect we will find magnificently preserved structures up to one or two stories high."

Researchers are now directing their attention to two key aspects of Nabataean society. Some are attempting to learn about the Nabataeans' religious beliefs and rituals, while others are focusing on the details of everyday life: how ordinary people earned their livings and what their homes and families were like.

Little is known about the life of the city after Roman times, but the most spectacular discovery in Petra in recent years is casting new light on the city's Byzantine period. In 1990, an archaeologist from the American Center for Oriental Research (ACOR) in Amman, Jordan, unearthed the floor and partial walls of a Byzantine church from the 6th century. The floor is decorated with two mosaics, each about 72 feet square. They depict animals such as elephants and giraffes, symbols of the seasons, a fisherman, a camel driver, and a flute player. These mosaics are now being cleaned and restored. One of the most significant finds in the church is a set of about 40 scrolls. Scientists estimate that they are more than 1,400 years old and could date back to late Roman times. Although the scrolls are badly burned, they still can be read in spots. Scholars are working to decipher their contents, which appear to be written in Byzantine Greek and another script that has not yet been identified.

Archaeologists are also attempting to answer one of the most perplexing questions about Petra: Why was it abandoned? Even after it lost its hold over the caravan trade, Petra could have survived as a city. Why didn't it? Natural disasters may have contributed to Petra's downfall. A severe earthquake struck Petra in A.D. 363. After the quake, many structures remained in ruins, their owners unable or unwilling to restore them. "If you look at the shops along the colonnaded streets, you see that many shopkeepers simply rebuilt their structures in front of those that had collapsed in the earthquake, rather than bothering to clear away the rubble," said Zbiegniew Fiema, part of the ACOR team that is excavating the Byzantine church. "It is a sign that the wealth and order of the city was beginning to decline." Petra was rocked by another severe quake in 551. That quake probably knocked down the Byzantine church; the scrolls in the church may have been burned in fires that swept through the city after the quake.

Yet many cities have been rebuilt on ruins after earthquakes and fires. Why not Petra? In 1991, in a book called *Packrat Middens,* a team of scientists from Arizona proposed an answer. They had studied the middens, or dens, of packrats and hyraxes, small rodents that collect sticks, plants, bones, and dung. The animals' dens become saturated with their urine, and chemicals in the urine then harden into a cementlike substance, preventing the contents of the middens from decaying. Some of these middens have been found to be 40,000 years old. Each midden is like a time capsule from the past, filled with samples of vegetation and pollen from the period in which the midden was made.

After studying a series of hyrax middens at Petra, the scientists discovered that in early Nabataean times, an oak and pistachio wood-

In 1990 archaeologists at Petra unearthed ruins of a Byzantine church that may have been destroyed in an earthquake in 551. Scholars hope to decipher some badly burned scrolls found in the ruins.

land covered the slopes around Petra. By Roman times, however, much of this forest had vanished; the cutting of timber for building and firewood had turned the area into an open steppe-land of shrubs and grasses. The process continued until, by A.D. 900, the shrubs and grasses were disappearing because of intensive grazing by goats, and the region was well on its way to becoming desert. The scientists suggest that environmental degradation was a factor in Petra's decline: The city died when its surroundings could no longer produce enough food and fuel for a large population.

Petra is like a book of which only the first few pages have been read. Not far from the Byzantine church Fiema noticed a granite column sticking up out of the ground. "Granite is not available in Jordan," he explained to an interviewer. "It must have come from Egypt. I often look at that column and wonder what structure lies beneath the ground. Is it a royal palace? A temple? Wherever you walk in Petra, you are faced with such puzzles."

Research in the coming decades will tell us much more about all stages in Petra's history, from prehistory to the age of Islam. "The city of Petra has hardly been touched, and we expect to find many surprises," said the director of ACOR in 1994. "This is a first-class site, and one of the great archaeological treasures of the Middle East."

People of the ancient world—as well as birds, horses, and other animals—are pictured in the floor mosaics of Petra's Byzantine church, shown in an aerial view.

CHAPTER 2

Nineveh

Secrets of Ancient Assyria

A s 19th-century Europeans and Americans became more interested in the remote past, one region exerted a special allure: Mesopotamia, "the land between the rivers." Bordered by the Tigris and Euphrates Rivers, Mesopotamia— now contained within the modern nation of Iraq—was known to have been the homeland of ancient civilizations that are mentioned in the writings of Greek historians and in the Old Testament of the Bible. Europeans were particularly fascinated by the sophisticated, decadent Babylonians and the fierce, warlike Assyrians. Although only a crumbling mound remained at the site, the location of ancient Babylon was well known. But what about other ancient cities, such as Nineveh? This mighty Assyrian city was described in the Bible as the capital of Sennacherib, a king who made war upon the Jewish kingdoms of Israel and Judah. But where in Mesopotamia could it be found?

Since the 16th century, Mesopotamia had been part of the Ottoman Empire. It was, in fact, a sleepy backwater of that empire, largely

After Nineveh was unearthed in 1847, an artist drew this reconstruction of what Nineveh's palace might have looked like. One object found among the ruins was this ivory carving of a cow and her calf.

neglected by its overlords in Constantinople (present-day Istanbul). The few outsiders who wandered into Mesopotamia found themselves beset by bandits and quarrelsome chieftains, as well as by corrupt governors and other local officials who demanded bribes. Scorching desert heat, prowling lions, and virulent diseases such as cholera and dysentery also made Mesopotamian travel a hazardous venture. Nevertheless, a few hardy and curious souls took the risk and explored sites renowned in ancient legend and history.

One of the first of these adventurers was an Italian named Pietro della Valle, who entered Mesopotamia in 1616. He returned unscathed to Europe with souvenirs from the ruins of Babylon, including the first samples of a new kind of writing that Europeans had ever seen. This writing, which consisted of wedge-shaped marks on tablets of dried clay, came to be called cuneiform (literally, wedge-form) script.

In 1756, the king of Denmark sent a six-man scientific expedition to the Middle East. Five of the six perished of disease, but Carsten Niebuhr managed to make his way to Persepolis, the 2,000-year-old capital of the ancient Persians in what is now Iran. He returned to Europe with copies of cuneiform inscriptions he found at Persepolis. Published in 1772, these inscriptions provided valuable clues to the scholars who later struggled to decode the cuneiform script. One of the languages used in the inscriptions turned out to be Old Persian, which was already fairly well known in other types of script. In the early 1800s, researchers began to decipher the cuneiform version of Old Persian.

Meanwhile, the European powers had decided to establish closer trade and diplomatic links with the Ottoman Empire. In 1802, Britain stationed a formal representative called a consul in Mesopotamia. Six years later 22-year-old Claudius James Rich took over the post. Rich was a scholar as well as a diplomat; he was deeply interested in ancient history and relics. During his consulship, the British residency in Baghdad became a center of archaeological activity.

Rich drew sketches of the ruins of Babylon, collected cuneiform tablets there, and published several scholarly papers about Babylon and his researches. Babylon was not Rich's only interest, however. He also dreamed of finding the lost city of Nineveh, and in 1820 he examined two mounds across the Tigris River from the town of Mosul, north of Baghdad. Atop the mound called Kuyunjik he found broken pottery and mud bricks with cuneiform inscriptions. But before Rich could begin excavating the mound, he died of cholera while caring for victims of an epidemic of that disease in Persia.

Rich's widow sold his collection of cuneiform inscriptions to the British Museum in London, and soon scholars from many countries were puzzling over copies of them. The breakthrough in deciphering cuneiform came not in a quiet museum library, however, but in a rocky gorge in Persia. It was made by Henry Creswicke Rawlinson. Rawlinson was a soldier and sportsman who made himself into a scholar. His interest in cuneiform began in 1835, when military duties took him to the small town of Behistun in Persia. He heard rumors of rock carvings nearby and went to have a look. To his surprise, Rawlinson found himself staring at a vast carved panel 340 feet up a sheer cliff. It depicted Darius, a king of the ancient Persians, preparing to punish rebel warlords. Around and below the figures was a lengthy cuneiform inscription of 1,200 lines in three languages. Aware that the inscriptions might provide a vital key to the understanding

A broken tile shows Ashurnasirpal II, king of the Assyrians in the 9th century B.C., holding a cup of wine. The bodyguards behind him are armed with bows and arrows.

Through luck and daring, soldier-turned-scholar Henry Rawlinson obtained the vital clue that allowed scholars to read the languages of ancient Mesopotamia.

of the cuneiform script, Rawlinson repeatedly risked his life on narrow ledges and rickety ladders to copy them. The most inaccessible part of the inscription was copied by a Kurdish boy whom Rawlinson paid to be hauled across the rock face in a rope sling.

By the time he had acquired a complete copy of the inscription, Rawlinson had become the British consul in Baghdad. There he settled down to solve the mysteries of cuneiform. Working under an artificial waterfall he had created to keep cool in the blistering heat, with his pet lion cub curled at his feet, he compared the three versions of the text. Soon he had succeeded in deciphering the Old Persian version, but the other two languages baffled him at first. Within a few years, however, he had succeeded in cracking one of the unknown languages. It was Babylonian, the language of a culture that had arisen in Mesopotamia thousands of years earlier. This had been the language not only of the ancient Babylonians, but of the Assyrians as well.

In 1851, Rawlinson published his translation of the Babylonian part of the Behistun inscription. Mesopotamian archaeology had taken a great step forward. Now scores of Babylonian inscriptions waited to be translated. Yet the third language continued to perplex the cuneiformists. Scholars eventually called it Elamite, after an ancient Persian people. Meanwhile, in 1869 a French scholar named Jules Oppert suggested that the cuneiform method had been invented in Sumer, in southern Mesopotamia, and adopted by later people, including the Elamites and the Babylonians. Modern scholars have determined that Oppert was right. Sumerian is the oldest known written language and the source of the cuneiform script used by a number of later cultures in the Middle East.

Mesopotamia was beginning to yield its buried secrets. While Rawlinson studied his inscriptions, working at deciphering Babylonian, others were digging into mounds and hillsides. One such searcher was Paul Emile Botta, the French consul at Mosul. Botta started to excavate at Kuyunjik, hoping to find the ruins of Nineveh, but lost interest when several months of work turned up only a few bricks. Then Botta heard about a place called Khorsabad, just a few miles north, said to be rich in inscribed bricks. He sent a few workmen to investigate. They returned with wild stories of walls bearing huge images of men and monsters.

Botta rushed off to Khorsabad, where he saw that his workers had unearthed wall carvings of bearded men and of bulls and lions with wings and human heads. The delighted Botta announced to the world that he had found Nineveh. The French government ordered him to remove as many relics as possible and send them to Paris. This proved a difficult task, but not an impossible one.

Unlike the ruins of Greece, Rome, and Egypt, which are made of stone, the ancient cities of Mesopotamia were built of sun-dried mud brick. Only statues, important gateways, and ceremonial or decorative wall panels were made of stone. Because the bricks of the Mesopotamian cities tended to crumble or erode over time, early investigators had a hard time tracing the outlines of particular buildings. The sites they excavated looked less like buried cities than like huge anthills, piles of dirt and crumbled brick into which they bored tunnels in search of treasure, tablets, or sculptures.

Botta's excavation at Khorsabad yielded many immense sculptures: human-headed winged bulls that had once guarded a palace gateway, 15-foot-tall alabaster portraits of gods and kings, and more. With enormous effort, Botta's crew of sweating workmen wrestled these trophies onto rafts on the Tigris River. They were floated downriver to the Persian Gulf and loaded aboard ships bound for France by way of the stormy waters around South Africa's Cape of Good Hope. Although some sculptures broke or were lost in the Tigris or at sea, a good number of Botta's finds made it to Paris, where they caused a sensation. They created not only the new science of Assyriology but also a new fashion called

Austen Henry Layard (atop the wall at right) supervises the removal of a 10-ton stone figure from the palace of Ashurnasirpal II in Nimrud. The statue was destined for a long journey to the British Museum, as European excavators raced to fill their countries' museums with the treasures of the Assyrians.

In an 1843 portrait, Layard wears a Persian headdress and robe. He spurned the life of a lawyer for adventure and archaeology—and perhaps a bit of espionage—in the Middle East.

"Assyrian revival," in which furniture, ornaments, jewelry, and women's clothing mirrored the designs found in an ancient Assyrian king's palace.

Determined not to let the French get all the credit for rediscovering Assyria, the British sent their own agent to Mesopotamia. His name was Austen Henry Layard. Trained as a lawyer in London, Layard was an adventurous young man who had traveled through much of the Middle East. He worked for the British consul in Constantinople on what one biographical source calls "various unofficial diplomatic missions"—something between espionage and politics. In 1845, the consul sent Layard to Mosul to stake Britain's claim to Assyriological glory.

Passing himself off to the suspicious French and the local chieftains as an innocent boar hunter, Layard smuggled some tools to a mound near Mosul and started digging. Before the day was out he and his workers had found the remains of two Assyrian palaces. Soon he turned up ivory carvings, cuneiform tablets, and sculptured panels of battle scenes. "I live among the ruins," he wrote home to an aunt, "and dream of little else."

Layard was certain that he, and not Botta, had found the site of Nineveh. Like Botta, he concentrated upon finding impressive items to ship home rather than upon a scientific exploration of the site. Soon enormous statues of winged lions and bulls, as well as other treasures, were making the difficult and perilous journey downriver. A single huge statue of a bull, surrounded by armed guards to fend off bandits, required a raft made of 600 goatskins. At the mouth of the Tigris, on the Persian Gulf, Layard's finds were transferred onto ships for the trip to London, where they reappeared in the stately halls of the British Museum.

In 1847, Layard began excavating at Kuyunjik, the mound that Botta had tested and then abandoned before making his big discovery at Khorsabad. Layard discovered that Botta had simply not dug deeply enough, for there was plenty to find 20 feet below the surface of Kuyunjik. In fact, as Henry Rawlinson soon proved by translating cuneiform texts, Kuyunjik really was the long-sought site of Nineveh. Layard's first site proved to be a city called Nimrud. Like Botta's site at Khorsabad, Nimrud had once been the capital of the Assyrian empire. But Nineveh was the legendary capital of Assyria's mightiest kings—the capital where, according to the Bible, the prophet Jonah had preached.

Over the course of several years, Layard made remarkable finds at Nineveh. He exposed part of a palace built by King Sennacherib, who ruled the Assyrians from 704 to 681 B.C. This structure included 71 rooms, one of which was a library later built by Sennacherib's grandson, King Ashurbanirpal. The library contained texts dealing with the language, medicine, religion, history, and literature of ancient Assyria. The palace also had at least 27 massive gateways, each flanked by huge stone bulls, lions, or sphinxes. Most impressive of all, perhaps, were the sculpted stone wall panels with scenes from Assyria's history and mythology. Layard calculated that if the panels he had found were laid end to end they would extend nearly two miles.

Layard retired from excavation in 1851, annoyed by the stingy sums doled out to him by the British Museum. Archaeological work in Mesopotamia continued sporadically under Arab, Iraqi, French, German, British, and American excavators. Some excavators spoke high-mindedly of the quest for knowledge; others were little more than glorified tomb robbers. Not until the 20th century did the scientific exploration of Nineveh, Nimrud, and the other cities of ancient Mesopotamia begin. Yet the 19th century brought another remarkable discovery from the land where history and the Bible seemed intertwined.

Beginning in the 1850s, researchers at the British Museum spent years sorting and translating the

A carved stone monument called the Black Obelisk, found in the ruins of Nimrud, shows scenes honoring Shalmaneser III, who ruled Assyria from 858 to 824 B.C. The figures in the pictures offer gifts to the king.

The Flood Tablet caused a stir in the 19th century. Scholars discovered that the tablet, which dates from the 7th century B.C., tells a story very similar to the biblical tale of Noah's Ark.

more than 24,000 cuneiform tablets that Layard had recovered from Nineveh. One of the most successful translators was an enthusiastic young Assyriologist named George Smith. One day Smith was examining a stack of broken tablets when he began reading something he could scarcely believe. It was an account in ancient Babylonian of heavy rains and a flood sent by the gods to punish sinful humans. A man named Utnapishtim had survived the flood by building a wooden boat, into which he loaded not only his own family but also a number of animals. Smith realized that he was reading a story very much like the story of the Flood and Noah's Ark, told in the Bible's Book of Genesis.

Smith's announcement of his find caused a sensation. Some people claimed that the tablet proved that the story of Noah's Ark was true. Others argued that the tablet showed that the Bible story was a legend based on a much older piece of mythology. But the Flood Tablet, as the cuneiform text came to be called, was broken, so Smith was unable to supply a full reading of the Babylonian story.

A London newspaper called the *Daily Telegraph* then sent Smith to Nineveh to look for the rest of the tablet. In what must rank as one of the luckiest coincidences of all time, Smith came across the missing piece of the tablet after less than a week in Nineveh. The newly restored lines of text added little to the story of the flood, however, and Smith—who had hoped to continue excavating—died of dysentery in Syria two years later.

We have learned a great deal about ancient Mesopotamia since the time of Botta and Layard. Even more than the excavation of the lost Mesopotamian cities, the translation of thousands of cuneiform documents has filled in many details about the Sumerians, Babylonians, and Assyrians.

Ancient Sumer was followed by two powerful civilizations, Babylon and Assyria. These two civilizations arose in Mesopotamia around 2000 B.C., with Babylon in the south and Assyria in the north. For a few centuries Babylon was the more powerful, but sometime around 1600 B.C. both peoples were conquered by invaders from outside Mesopotamia. After the invaders were driven out in the 14th century B.C., Assyria captured Babylon. During the 12th century Assyria flourished under a powerful king named Tiglath-pileser I, but Assyrian power faded after his death. Between 883 and 627 B.C., Assyria reclaimed its former glory under such leaders as King Sennacherib and King Ashurbanirpal.

It was Sennacherib who made Nineveh the capital of the Assyrian empire. The city was built on a hill and surrounded by a wall more than seven and a half miles in length, broken by at least five gates; there may have been more gates, but, if so, they have not been excavated. At the highest point of the hill, Sennacherib built his imperial palace, which covered two and a half acres. To build this monument to his magnificence, the Assyrian monarch imported skilled workers from Turkey, Persia, and Babylon. With them came rare materials such as scented woods, ivory, gold, silver, and white limestone. The palace was surrounded by lush, well-watered gardens. Inside were comfortable rooms. An elaborate system of wells, pulleys, and buckets supplied water to the king's bathroom, which had a shower; grilles and ventilators carried fresh air into the building; and a movable furnace on wheels provided heat during cold spells. Sennacherib's grandson Ashurbanirpal created the palace's impressive library and collected texts from every part of the world known to the Assyrians. For example, Ashurbanirpal ordered a subject in Babylon to "seek out and send to me any rare tablets which are known to you and are lacking in Assyria."

After Ashurbanirpal died in 627, Assyria once again grew weak. Soon invaders from Persia and Babylon captured Nineveh. King Nebuchadnezzar of Babylon defeated the last remnants of the Assyrian army in 605 B.C., and Assyria disappeared into the dust of history. The Hebrew prophet Zephaniah, whose people had been oppressed by the Assyrians, rejoiced in Nineveh's downfall: "See what has befallen the joyous city who queened it without a care, and said in her heart, 'There is none like me.' How she has become a desert, a resort for the wild beasts! Whoever shall pass by her will hiss and wave his hand." Several generations of adventurers, archaeologists, and scholars, however, have revealed Nineveh's vanished glories to the modern world.

CHAPTER 3

Hattusha
The Citadel of the Hittites

Adventurous wandering scholars such as Johann Ludwig Burckhardt and Claudius James Rich set a new fashion in travel in the early 19th century. For some time, people from England and western Europe had been content to make what they called "the Grand Tour"—a trip around Europe, perhaps going as far south as Naples and as far east as Greece. But now Europeans—and Americans, too, such as John Lloyd Stephens—began visiting western Asia and North Africa in significant numbers. Fired by accounts of Egypt and Petra, these travelers developed a passion for the ancient cities mentioned in the Bible and in old Greek and Roman chronicles. Nothing pleased them more than locating the buried or forgotten ruins of such a place. Antiquarians, as people with an interest in the relics of antiquity were called, made many mistakes by modern standards. When exploring ruins, they dug trenches and moved artifacts without making any records of what they had done, hopelessly contaminating the work of later, more careful, investigators. Even worse, they were generally insensitive to the claims of the local inhabitants—or just plain

These ruins in central Turkey puzzled early archaeologists. The ruins were the first clue to the existence of the Hittites, makers of this silver cup in the shape of a bull's head.

greedy. Some looted sites for valuable treasure. Others did the same thing in the pursuit of scholarship, hauling off museum-loads of artifacts, including monuments, statues, and sometimes whole buildings, to London, Paris, Berlin, and, later, New York. At the same time, however, the antiquarians of the 18th and 19th centuries laid the foundations of the modern science of archaeology.

In 1834, Charles Felix-Marie Texier (1802–71), a French architect, artist, and antiquarian, was traveling in Anatolia, the large peninsula east of the Aegean Sea that was known to the Romans as Asia Minor and is today the nation of Turkey. Anatolia is one of the world's great crossroads. It lies between Asia to the east, Europe and the Mediterranean Sea to the west, Mesopotamia to the south, and the steppes of Russia to the north. For centuries armies had crisscrossed the Anatolian plain, traders had carried goods across it from one end of the world to the other, cultures had met there and mixed.

Texier and his learned contemporaries knew that the Romans had established colonies in Anatolia, and that before the Romans the armies of the Greeks and the Persians had battled there. Their ideas of Anatolia's history extended back to the mid-500s B.C. Texier did not know that he was about to stumble upon the first clue to a much more ancient history.

Like other antiquarians of the day, Texier traveled across Turkey in search of places mentioned in Greek and Roman history. He hoped to locate Tavium, a Roman colony in central Anatolia. From village to village he went, asking peasants if they knew of any local ruins. In the north-central part of Anatolia, at the Turkish village of Bogazköy—today called Boghazkeui—Texier felt that he was nearing his goal. To his delight, the villagers told him that there were ruins on the mountainside behind Bogazköy.

The villagers led Texier up into the hills, and there were the promised ruins. Texier was startled. The ruins were grander and more extensive than he had expected. Remains of an old city wall enclosed an area of more than 300 acres. Parts of the wall were still standing, including two enormous gateways; one gateway was flanked by a pair of stone lions, and the other bore a large carved sphinx.

That was not all, the villagers told Texier. They led him northeast along a mountain path. After an hour, Texier saw some tall outcroppings of limestone rock looming in front of him. As he drew closer, he saw that the outcroppings were split by deep clefts that formed natural, roofless passages and chambers. The walls of these tall chambers, Texier discovered, were carved into dozens of sculptures of men and women who appeared to be kings and queens, gods and goddesses. The villagers told Texier that they called the place Yazilikaya, which meant "inscribed rocks."

Texier was perplexed. Had he found Tavium? He decided that he had not. The style of the sculptures at Bogazköy and Yazilikaya, together with the heavy, massive look of the ruins, convinced the knowledgeable Texier that the site was not Roman after all. "No building here could be attributed to any Roman period," he wrote in *Description of Asia Minor*, which was published in Paris in 1839. "I was extraordinarily disconcerted by the grandiose and singular nature of the ruins as I sought to give the city its historical name." Texier decided that the city might have been Pteria, a city in Anatolia mentioned by the ancient Greek historian Herodotus. According to Herodotus, Pteria was destroyed in a battle in 547 B.C. Not until well after Texier's death would archaeologists discover that Bogazköy and Yazilikaya were much older than that. Solving the riddle of Texier's ruins would prove to be a long-drawn-out, painstaking process that would require the contributions of half a dozen scholars and clues from all over the ancient world.

The next European to see Texier's ruins was William Hamilton of Britain's Royal Geological Society, who visited Turkey several times. He sketched the carvings of Yazilikaya in 1840. Hamilton was impressed by the number of ruins to be found on the Anatolian plateau. "There is scarcely a spot of ground however small that does not contain some relic of antiquity," he said in 1842. Yet Hamilton believed that all those relics had been left by Greeks and Romans. Scornful of the Anatolian people, he did not believe that any great civilization could ever have arisen within Anatolia.

The question remained: Just who had created the buildings and carvings at Bogazköy and Yazilikaya? The answer was long in coming. It began to surface in 1872, when an Irish missionary named William Wright obtained five large blocks of carved stone from the Syrian town of Hama, where Johann Ludwig Burckhardt had noticed them 60 years earlier.

Wright hoped that the scholars at the British Museum would be able to decipher the symbols carved into the stones. Although Wright could not read the symbols, he thought that they might have been made by a mysterious people called the Hittites. The Hittites are mentioned several times in the Bible's Old Testament, but other than these few references they had left no mark on history. Some scholars doubted that such a people had even existed.

The next piece of the puzzle fell into place in 1879, when a British scholar named Archibald Sayce compared photographs of Texier's findings at Bogazköy and Yazilikaya with photographs of the Hama stones. Some of the symbols, Sayce found, were identical. This suggested that a single civilization had stretched from north-central Anatolia to Syria, hundreds of miles to the south. By this time, other scholars working on Assyrian and Egyptian documents had found references to a civilization called "the people of Hatti." Sayce decided that the "people of Hatti" could be the same as those called Hittites in the Bible. Furthermore, Sayce suggested, they could have built the hilltop citadel near Bogazköy. But the Hittites had not yet emerged from the murky realm of myth into the light of history.

The key to unraveling the mysteries of the Hittites was found not in Turkey, but in faraway Egypt. In 1887, a number of clay tablets covered with cuneiform writing were discovered at the Egyptian village of Tell al-'Amarna. This remarkable find turned out to illuminate not only Egyptian history but Hittite history as well.

The Amarna tablets were administrative records from the court of the pharaoh Akhenaton, who ruled Egypt in the 14th century B.C. Many of them mentioned the "people of Hatti"—the Hittites. Almost all of the Amarna tablets were written in cuneiform, in Akkadian, a language that was well known to 19th-century scholars. Two of them, however, were written in an unknown language that baffled the philologists, or language specialists, who examined them.

In 1893, a French anthropologist named Ernest Chantre did a little digging at Bogazköy. He found pieces of two cuneiform tablets written in the same baffling language as the indecipherable Amarna tablets. This find established a definite link between ancient Egypt and whatever civilization had built the Bogazköy citadel. Scholars began to propose theories about the Hittites—especially after more references to this mysterious people came to light in newly translated Egyptian documents from the 15th through the 12th centuries B.C.

At Yazilikaya an ancient people carved dozens of regal and godlike figures into natural rock walls. The carvings were neither Greek nor Roman. Who made them? The answer was long in coming.

In 1905, one of the Bogazköy tablets was sent to a scholar named Hugo Winckler, an expert in Babylonian and Assyrian cuneiform at Berlin University. Winckler was determined to solve the mystery of the unknown language, which he suspected was Hittite. With the help of Theodore Makridi, a Turkish official from the Ottoman Museum in Constantinople, he began excavating at Bogazköy in 1906.

Winckler seems to have been a rather disagreeable man: jealous of other people's success, intolerant of opinions that differed from his own. He complained endlessly about the everyday inconveniences of the journey to Bogazköy, such as bad weather and bedbugs. And once at the site, he completely ignored the principle of stratigraphy—the careful noting of the layers, or strata, in which objects are found underground.

Taking their cue from geologists, archaeologists had begun to realize that stratigraphy could help them establish the history of a site according to the simple principle that deeper layers are older and upper layers are more recent. Stratigraphy provided an extremely useful tool, but it demanded time and patience: Excavators had to proceed slowly, recording the location of every find in each layer before digging down to the next layer. But Winckler sat himself down under a shade tree and paid the villagers to dig however they pleased. His only interest was in clay tablets, and he did not care how they were obtained.

Reckless as his methods were, Winckler did get impressive results when the diggers began unearthing tablets. He realized at once that he was dealing with two groups of tablets. Some were written in the Babylonian language, which he read with ease, and others were written in the unknown language. Clearly, the Bogazköy site had been an important city in some vanished civilization. But was it the Hittite civilization? On 20 August 1906, Winckler found the answer. One of the workers brought him a tablet inscribed in Babylonian cuneiform. "One look at it, and all the experience of my life paled into insignificance," Winckler later wrote.

The tablet Winckler's digger had found was a copy of a text that had recently become familiar to all archaeologists. It was a peace treaty made in 1270 B.C. between Ramses II, pharaoh of Egypt, and Hattushili III, emperor of the

Hittites. A copy of the treaty in Egyptian hieroglyphs was carved into a temple wall at Karnak, Egypt. Now Winckler was looking at another copy of the treaty. Such things were kept only in the official archives of the nations concerned, which meant that Bogazköy must be the long-sought Hittite capital. Winckler's speculations, and those of Sayce before him, were confirmed. The elusive Hittites had at last been pinned down—in Turkey.

Winckler and Makridi continued to excavate tablets from Bogazköy until Winckler's death in 1912. Altogether Winckler found about 10,000 tablets or parts of tablets. Yet he never succeeded in deciphering the Hittite language. That achievement was the work of a Czech scholar named Bedrich Hrozny, who announced in 1915 that he had made a breakthrough in decoding the Hittite tablets. Hrozny had recognized that Hittite was related not to the Middle Eastern languages, but to the Indo-European languages of India and Europe. By the mid-1940s, scholars had gained a fairly complete understanding of all forms of the written Hittite language.

Even before Winckler's death in 1912, another team of German archaeologists had begun excavating and mapping the ancient city's walls, temples, and palaces. Work at the site was interrupted by World War I (1914–18) and again by World War II (1939–45). Since the 1950s, archaeological work at Bogazköy has been continued, largely by German and Turkish expeditions. Their discoveries have brought the total number of clay tablets recovered at Bogazköy to more than 25,000, including more than 3,000 that the German archaeologist Peter Neve uncovered in a royal archive in 1990–91. But although the Hittites have now taken their place in history, much remains to be learned about their origins, their empire, and their ultimate fate.

Long before the Hittites, people were living on the Anatolian plateau. Archaeologists now know that Turkey's rich and complex history stretches back for thousands of years before the Persians, Greeks, and Romans. Prehistoric sites on the Anatolian plateau are among the oldest known

In 1640 B.C., the first Hittite king, Hattushili, addressed these words to his heir: "You must keep my words. As long as you keep them, Hattusha will stand tall, and you will make your land be at peace." They were preserved on a clay tablet found at Hattusha.

settlements in the world, dating back to 7000 B.C. or earlier. Over the centuries, various cultures rose and fell; these early Anatolian cultures are now the subject of much study. By 1950 B.C., a settlement or fortress existed on the Bogazköy site. It was called Hattush by its inhabitants, who referred to the region as "the land of Hatti."

Sometime in the late 18th century B.C., Hattush was destroyed in a war between the Hatti people and a warlike people who had migrated into the region. Modern scholars are not sure where these newcomers came from or whether they arrived in a slow trickle or in a sudden mass migration. One band of the newcomers attacked and leveled Hattush; their leader pronounced a curse on anyone who dared to settle the site again. Within a century, however, a warlord of one of the new tribes had rebuilt Hattush, renamed it Hattusha, and made it his capital. He changed his name from Labarnas to Hattushila, meaning "king of Hattusha." King Hattushila founded a dynasty, or ruling family, that was the beginning of the Hittite kingdom. His people came to be known as Hittites, or "people of Hatti"—a rare example of a conquering people taking on the name of their vanquished foes.

A stone tablet imprinted with the royal seal of the Hittite king Tudhalija IV. The king ruled in the mid-13th century B.C., a generation or two before the fall of the Hittite civilization.

Unlike the original Hattians, the Hittites were an aggressive people who soon extended their domain over much of central Anatolia, where archaeologists have found numerous other Hittite sites. The Hittites also ventured farther afield. In the mid-16th century B.C., a Hittite king conquered Syria, south of Anatolia, and then led his army 500 miles farther south to conquer the Mesopotamian capital of Babylon. Diverted by troubles back in Anatolia, however, the Hittites soon withdrew from Babylon and returned to their homeland.

Over the next few centuries, the Hittites engaged in both royal intermarriage and periodic warfare with Egypt. In 1246 B.C., King Hattushili III sent one of his daughters to Egypt to marry the pharaoh Ramses. A carving on the wall of a temple at Abu Simbel, Egypt shows the meeting of the Egyptian pharaoh and the Hittite princess.

To defend the Anatolian homeland and to carry out wars of conquest abroad, the Hittite kings maintained large armies of up to 30,000 soldiers who fought with axes, swords, and bows. The Hittites were noted for their ironwork; the forges of Hattusha turned out high-quality iron tools, weapons, and armor. The Hittites' most effective weapon, however, was the chariot. In a tactic that terrified their opponents, Hittite charioteers drove their iron-studded chariots right into the ranks of advancing soldiers.

The heart of Hattusha was a hilltop fortress or citadel that was easy to defend because it was protected on two sides by steep crags. The Hittites built thick, tall, sloping walls to protect the other approaches to this citadel, which contained the royal palace. In the 1950s a team of German researchers led by archaeologist Kurt Bittel discovered the quarters of the king and queen in the northwest corner of the citadel. The citadel also contained the imperial archives; most of the clay tablets have been found in this part of the city. Sometime after 1400 B.C., Hattusha was greatly enlarged by the building of a curving four-mile-long wall that extended its boundaries in several directions. The wall carvings and a temple at Yazilikaya also date from around this time.

A gate into Hattusha's hilltop citadel, which contained the royal palace of the Hittites.

Hittite society was rigidly divided into classes, with the king and queen at the top. The monarch's powers were not absolute, however; royal actions were overseen by a panel of nobles. The nobles occupied the next level of society. One level down were the generals and court officials. Below them were the merchants and the artisans, such as blacksmiths and potters. Lower still were the farmers who produced the wheat, barley, honey, and fruit that fed the city. At the bottom were the slaves. All were governed by a detailed code of written laws that defined punishments for murder, rape, treason, and other crimes.

If Hittite laws were strict, they were also fair. The laws reflect a sense of balance. Cruel punishments such as torture were outlawed. Instead, the punishment for most crimes called for the criminal to make some form of repayment to those who had been wronged. A murderer, for example, had to pay blood money to the victim's family. Like nearly every other civilization of the time, the Hittites kept slaves—usually prisoners of war. Slaves did have some rights in Hittite society, however. They could own property and purchase their freedom.

Women in the Hittite empire enjoyed rights and freedoms that were unknown to the women of Mesopotamia and Egypt. Hittite law gave them the right to practice professions as the equals of men. Documents and royal seals suggest that the Hittite queens and kings ruled as partners. On occasion the empire was ruled by a queen alone.

The Hittites were a religious people—but, unlike some other ancient civilizations, they were tolerant of the beliefs of others. The Hittites have been called "people of a thousand gods" because they allowed the worship of Syrian, Babylonian, and other gods and even incorporated these deities into the Hittite pantheon. Archaeologists have found traces of 31 temples in Hattusha. The largest and best-preserved of these is called the Great Temple. It is a complex of structures and passageways that covers five acres and probably once housed more than 200 priests, clerks, musicians, and other servants of the gods. In 1962, archaeologists found in one of the storerooms of the Great Temple a tablet that suggests that the temple was dedicated to the worship of the weather god and the sun goddess. These were the supreme Hittite deities. During the later centuries of the Hittite empire, the king himself came to be considered a god.

The Hittite civilization flourished for more than half a millennium. But around 1200 B.C. disaster struck. Scientists have found evidence that within a span of only a few years, Hattusha and many other Hittite cities were burned to the ground. Although the overthrow of the Hittites was swift and sudden, the conditions that led to it had been developing for decades. It appears that a series of bad harvests—brought about by a centuries-long drought that affected the entire Middle East—weakened the empire. Scholars believe that this prolonged drought created chaos and instability throughout the region, causing whole peoples to migrate in search of better conditions. Hattusha and the rest of the Hittite empire appear to have been overthrown by a combination of invading peoples from the west, marauding nomads from the north, and restless subject peoples who chafed under Hittite rule.

By 1150 B.C., the Hittite empire was no more. Those Hittites who survived the destruction of their cities fled in all directions and, over time, were probably assimilated into other peoples. But the Hittites left a footnote in history. About 200 years after the fall of the Hittite empire, a group of small kingdoms arose in eastern Anatolia and northern Syria. Archaeologists believe that the people of these kingdoms were not descended from the Hittites. They adopted the Hittite language, however, and borrowed some of the Hittites' deities and customs. Scholars call these kingdoms the Neo-Hittites, or New Hittites.

In Syria, the Neo-Hittites set up city-states that survived until about the 8th century B.C. These Syrian Neo-Hittites carved the Hama stones that William Wright found in Syria. The Neo-Hittites were also mentioned in the Bible. The Hama stones and the scattered biblical references were among the first clues that helped modern scholars unravel the mystery of the Hittites—those, and the enigmatic stone ruins found on a Turkish hillside by Charles Texier.

A sphinx from the south gate of Hattusha's imperial quarter. The Egyptians and other ancient peoples also created images of sphinxes, mythical creatures with human heads and animal bodies.

CHAPTER 4

Copán
Mysteries of the Maya

Two travelers, an Englishman and an American, made their way into the rain forest of Central America in 1839. Directed by local guides, they inched along muddy muletracks that crept upward into the rugged highlands of Honduras. This green world of tangled tree roots and dripping leaves, of white butterflies and croaking tree frogs, would have fascinated a biologist, but the two travelers had not come to Honduras to study rare plants or strange animals. They were looking for a lost city called Copán.

The Englishman was a 40-year-old artist and experienced traveler named Frederick Catherwood. In the age before photography, artists played a vital role in scientific expeditions; their illustrations both recorded and publicized new discoveries. Catherwood had worked for an archaeological expedition in Egypt and had produced some much-admired drawings and paintings of ruins in the Near East. The American was 34-year-old John Lloyd Stephens, who had grown up in a prosperous family, become a lawyer, and given up his business to travel for several years in

In its prime, the Mayan city of Copán boasted huge pyramids and a sweeping plaza, later swallowed by the Central American jungle. Copán and other sites have yielded thousands of artifacts, including this painted bowl.

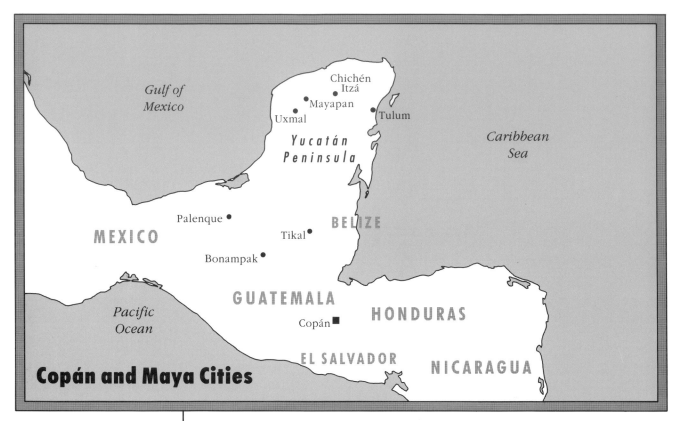

Copán and Maya Cities

Europe, Russia, the Near East, Arabia, and Egypt. Shortly before returning to the United States in 1836, Stephens met Catherwood in London. Drawn together by their interest in ruins and ancient civilizations, the two men became friends. Soon Catherwood moved with his family to New York City, where Stephens lived, and the two began planning an expedition. Although Catherwood was not prosperous, Stephens had made a small fortune from the sales of *Incidents of Travel in Arabia Petraea,* a book he published in 1837 that described his travels in the Near East and his visits to such sites as the ancient city of Petra. The income from this book would help pay for the new expedition.

The explorers decided to make Central America their goal. Although large ruins were known to exist in southern Mexico, the Yucatán Peninsula, Guatemala, and Honduras, very little was known about these relics. The Spanish conquistadors and the generations of Spanish missionaries and colonial officials who followed them to the New World had left accounts of the Aztec civilization they encountered in the central valley of Mexico and of the Inca empire in South America. The Spanish chroniclers, however, had not paid much attention to the lands and peoples that lay between their two richest American colonies.

A few 16th- and 17th-century priests did study the people called the Maya, the farmers and fishers who lived in Yucatán, Honduras, and Guatemala when the Spanish arrived. The priests' efforts, however, were directed at Christianizing the Maya—by wiping out their native language and religion. One of the most earnest of these missionary priests was Diego de Landa, who tortured thousands of Indians in the name of Christ. To justify Spain's treatment of the Maya, Landa made a close study of their culture, which he deemed barbaric and superstitious. He recognized that the Maya possessed a written alphabet; indeed, he copied some symbols from it in one of his chronicles. Landa believed, however, that Maya books were worthless, even evil. Once he came upon 30 of these books: pounded tree bark, painted with plaster to create a smooth surface, covered with painted glyphs, or symbols, and then folded like fans. Modern archaeologists call these volumes codices. The ruthless Landa burned them, despite the protests of the anguished Indians.

Landa's writings, and those of other priests of his era, did include scattered references to lost cities, temples, or ruins in Maya country, but these accounts were ignored or buried in Spain's colonial archives. Not until the late 18th century did a few hardy travelers begin poking around the ruins. Antonio del Rio, an officer in the Mexican army, visited the ruins at Palenque in southern Mexico in 1786. Another officer, Guillermo Dupaix, returned to Palenque about 20 years later. Del Rio's and Dupaix's descriptions of the ruins were published in the early 19th century. The volumes in which they appeared, however, were obscure and failed to attract much attention from the world at large.

Athough he destroyed Mayan books whenever he found them, missionary Diego de Landa did make this record of the sounds that corresponded to certain Mayan symbols. Landa's notes helped 20th-century scholars "break the code" of the Mayan inscriptions he had scorned.

Traveler, writer, and archaeological explorer, John Lloyd Stephens believed that the ruins he found in Copán were "of a new order," the relics of a great civilization that had been born in the Americas.

Still, the curious continued to make their way to the ruins, although the journey was not for the faint of heart. Dupaix described the road to Palenque as "scarcely passable for any other animal than a bird . . . winding through mountains and over precipices." In the early 1830s, Juan Galindo, governor of northern Guatemala, took to those rough jungle tracks. He visited two sets of ruins, Palenque and Copán, and published a report about them. Around the same time, an adventurer named Jean Frederic Waldeck spent some months sketching the ruins at Palenque; his book, illustrated with many drawings, was published in 1838. Stephens read these tantalizing accounts and was surprised that they had not aroused more interest. He decided that he and Catherwood would be the ones to bring the little-known ruins of Central America to the attention of the world.

A few scholars had already proposed theories about the Incas, the Aztecs, and the Maya. The concept of civilization fascinated 19th-century scholars. From the very beginning of European colonization in the Americas, the vast majority of Europeans had thought of themselves as culturally, morally, and intellectually superior to the native Americans. They dismissed the Indian civilizations as primitive or barbaric. And yet they had to account for certain undeniably impressive features of these civilizations, such as mighty stone monuments, sophisticated artwork, and advanced astronomical and timekeeping skills. How had these elements of "high" civilization appeared among the "low" savages?

The Westerners sought an answer in a concept called diffusionism. According to the diffusionists, civilization did not arise spontaneously in various parts of the world; it spread outward from a single, inspired source. Therefore, any evidence of "high" culture that was found in the Americas could be traced back to an earlier civilization in the Old World. Eager diffusionists thrust forward a cluster of suggestions. The ruins that had been reported to exist in Central America must have been built by Egyptians, Vikings, Phoenicians, Welsh or Irish exiles, Romans, even refugees from the legendary city of Atlantis. Two Dutch scholars quarreled over the question. One claimed that the ancestors of the American Indians were Scandinavian. The other replied indignantly that anyone could see that the Indians were descended from the Scythians, a nomadic tribe who lived on the steppes around the Black Sea 2,500 years ago, although he failed to offer a convincing explanation of how the Scythians got to North America. During the 18th and early 19th centuries, many people believed that the American Indians were descended from the biblical Lost Tribes of Israel and thus were related to the Jews.

The few people who had actually seen the ruins in Central America shed no light on the issue of their builders' origins. Del Rio could not guess who had built them. Neither could Dupaix, but he was sure that it had not been the Maya Indians who lived in the area, for these people were too "primitive" to have descended from such a grand culture. Galindo, on the other hand, believed that world civilization had originated in Central America. Culture and civilization had then moved westward, to China, India, Mesopotamia, and eventually to Europe, by which time the Central American birthplace of civilization had fallen into barbarity. Waldeck offered another exotic theory. Obsessed with Hindus and elephants, he claimed that the lost civilization of Central America was an offshoot of

A stela, or carved pillar. Much of the Mayan writing that survives is found on the thousands of stelae that the Maya erected in their cities to honor their rulers and record their history.

the Hindu culture of India, and that many of the strange symbols carved on monuments at Palenque were really elephant heads. Thus, when Stephens and Catherwood hacked their way through the jungle on the road to Copán, they were also carving their way into a thicket of contradictory theories.

The two explorers reached the valley of Copán, today the site of the modern town of Copán Ruinas in western Honduras. They saw a river, and beyond it a long stone wall 100 feet high. The wall was broken in places, and trees and brush grew out of it, but still they recognized it for what it was: the remains of a colossal structure. "We ascended by large stone steps," Stephens later wrote, "in some places perfect, and in others thrown down by trees which had grown up between the crevices, and reached a terrace, the form of which it was impossible to make out, from the density of the forest in which it was enveloped." Although much of Copán had been all but swallowed up by the jungle, Stephens and Catherwood found a semicircular amphitheater made of cut stone, stone statues of jaguars rearing up on their hind legs, and huge carved stone heads in the masonry above. Ahead of them, the broken stairway climbed up and up to the top of a huge pyramid, an artificial mountain of stone. On its summit was a temple, fallen into ruin and smothered by the roots of a fig tree. All around stood stelae, or pillars of carved stone. Some of the carvings were pictures of people and animals; others were glyphs unlike any the two men had ever seen.

Stephens and Catherwood laboriously climbed to the top of the 100-foot-tall pyramid and sat looking out at a mass of other pyramids and ruins, half-covered by vegetation. The scene was one of desolation and mystery. Stephens compared Copán, lost in the jungle, to a shipwreck: "It lay before us like a shattered bark in the midst of the ocean, her masts gone, her name effaced, her crew perished, and none to tell whence she came, to whom she belonged, how long on her voyage, or what caused her destruction." The local Maya could not answer the travelers' questions about the ruins. "Who knows?" was their invariable response to the explorers' queries. But with the panorama of Copán before him, Stephens was sure of one thing. These ruins were the remains of an accomplished, highly developed civilization.

The two men spent several weeks at Copán, exploring, mapping, and sketching. They agreed that Copán was more fascinating than even the well-known pyramids of Egypt. Stephens would later recall:

> It is impossible to describe the interest with which I explored these ruins. The ground was entirely new; there were no guidebooks or guides; the whole was virgin soil. We could not see 10 yards before us, and never knew what we should stumble upon next. At one time we stopped to cut away branches and vines which covered the face of a monument, and then to dig around and bring to light a fragment, a sculptured corner of which protruded from the earth. I leaned over with breathless anxiety while the Indians worked, and an eye, an ear, a foot or a hand was disentombed; and when the machete rang against the chiselled stone, I pushed the Indians away, and cleared out the loose earth with my hands.

Alfred P. Maudslay, who spent the 1880s photographing the Mayan ruins. Maudslay compiled a valuable photographic record still used by scientists.

Thrilling as such moments of discovery were, Stephens was eager to see more ruins, so he and Catherwood continued on a far-ranging trip that took them through Guatemala into the Chiapas region of southern Mexico. The travelers saw Palenque and scores of other sites that they had been told about along the way—"great cities beyond the Vale of Mexico, buried in forests, ruined, desolate, without a name," as Stephens described them. Noting that the stelae at these sites bore many of the same glyphs they had seen at Copán, they concluded that the whole region had been occupied by a single people. Furthermore, Stephens wrote, the ruins were "different from the works of any other known people, of a new order . . . they stand alone." Rejecting the diffusionist theories that were so popular at the time, Stephens firmly insisted that the ruins were utterly American in origin and had been built by the not-so-distant ancestors of the Maya

In 1895, researchers began trying to reassemble a 72-step stairway covered with glyphs. The Hieroglyphic Stairway had collapsed, and its tumbled inscriptions were like an archaeological jigsaw puzzle with more than 30,000 pieces.

Indians who still inhabited the region. With this pronouncement, the modern field of Maya studies was born.

After returning to New York, Stephens and Catherwood published *Incidents of Travel in Central America, Chiapas, and Yucatan* (1841). In 1842, they went back to Yucatán to examine the Maya ruins at Chichén Itzá and elsewhere; the results of this trip appeared in *Incidents of Travel in Yucatan* (1843). Both books were widely read and did much to promote interest in the Maya. A few years later, Stephens and Catherwood again went to Central America, this time as officials of a company that was building a railway through Panama. Stephens contracted malaria and hepatitis and died at home in New York in 1852; Catherwood died two years later aboard a ship that sank in the Atlantic.

Serious archaeological work at Copan began in the 1890s, with a series of expeditions from Harvard's Peabody Museum; similar expeditions investigated other Maya sites, such as Chichén Itzá in Yucatán. At the same time, photographers and artists were busy capturing images of the ruins and the archaeologists at work. A retired Englishman named Alfred P. Maudslay came to Central America in 1881 and spent more than a decade photographing the Maya ruins at his own expense. His archives, including many images from Copán, are of great help to modern scientists who are trying to trace the changes that have occurred at the sites over the past century. Adela Breton, an English artist, produced scores of finely detailed drawings at Chichén Itzá between 1900 and 1908; her work, too, is regarded by today's archaeologists as an important reference.

For Stephens, Copán was a mass of unanswered questions, but since his time scientists have learned much about this ancient Maya city. The Copán dis-

The Peabody Museum's second expedition to Copán gets under way in 1892. Travelers since the time of the Spanish invaders were amazed to see the surefooted local porters carry large loads on steep, narrow paths.

trict is a river valley of about 80 square miles. Copán itself covers a bit more than nine square miles at the bottom of the valley. Within that area are about 3,500 grass-covered mounds, each the remains of an old structure. Another thousand or so mounds are sprinkled along the valley.

In the center of Copán is a 30-acre area that archaeologists call the Main Group: the cluster of large ruins seen by Stephens and Catherwood. The most important buildings, including the big pyramids, are set above their surroundings on a high platform of earth and stone. Several smaller pyramids, temples, courtyards, and other structures are arranged around this platform. Large plazas among the pyramids are dotted with stelae, some of which are 13 feet tall. At one end of the great central plaza is a ball court. Archaeologists still do not know exactly what games were once played in this court, and in courts like it throughout Mexico and Central America. Games using heavy rubber balls and stone hoops were apparently played by many peoples in the region; some archaeologists believe that the games had a religious significance and may have included the sacrifice of the losers. All around the ball court, the pyramids jut up like steep, severe hills of solid stone.

Maya structures elsewhere were built of limestone, but the Copán region does not contain much limestone, so its buildings were made of a greenish volcanic stone found in the region. Copán would have been more colorful in its heyday than it is today, for there is evidence that the sculptures and carvings were painted red and perhaps other colors as well. Although the stone from which Copán was built is durable, the building blocks were fastened together with mud instead of the limestone mortar used at other sites. Over the centuries, the mud washed away and the buildings began to collapse—a process helped along by occasional earthquakes. As a result, Copán was in even poorer shape than the other Maya ruins.

The ball court at Copán. Games played here with a rubber ball and stone hoops may have resembled basketball—except that they might have ended with a sacrifice to the gods.

Copán was just one of many centers of Maya civilization. Archaeologists divide the Maya domain into three zones. From south to north they are the highlands (the mountains of present-day Guatemala and western El Salvador and Honduras); the southern lowlands (where the hills of Guatemala, southern Mexico, and Belize flatten out into a broad plain); and the northern lowlands (the Yucatán Peninsula). Copán is located on the border between the highlands and the southern lowlands. Its mountainous geography is that of the highlands, but its closest cultural ties were with the great Maya cities of the southern lowlands, including Tikal and Palenque.

People began settling in the lush Copán valley around 1100 B.C. Maya civilization emerged in the 2nd century B.C., and around A.D. 250 it entered the period that scholars call the Classic Maya era. At this time the Maya began building large cities in a number of locations, including Copán. In the 5th century, a king named Blue-Quetzal-Macaw came to power in Copán (a quetzal is a tropical bird that was sacred to the Maya). He ordered the building of the first large temples. His descendants ruled Copán for 15 generations. Under this dynasty, Copán became one of the leading Classic Maya cities.

One celebrated king of Copán was Smoke-Jaguar, who ruled for nearly 70 years in the 7th century. During his reign Copán's territory expanded, possibly through wars of conquest. The city grew until its population numbered perhaps 20,000. A sort of suburban development accompanied this population growth. As the area around the central pyramids filled with new temples, plazas, and houses for the nobility, other residents moved out into the cornfields and built new clusters of dwellings there. Gradually the peasant farmers who had once lived and worked just outside the city were forced out of the arable bottomland of the valley and up onto its less fertile slopes. They adapted their agricultural techniques, building stone terraces to keep the soil from washing away in the heavy rains, but nonetheless their productivity began to fall.

Smoke-Jaguar's son, 18 Rabbit, ruled Copán for the first part of the 8th century, at which time the city controlled about 100 square miles of territory. He ordered the creation of many carvings and sculptures that recounted the history and glories of Copán. But 18 Rabbit met an inglorious end; he was captured and beheaded by the leader of a neighboring town. His successor, Smoke-Shell, tried to restore the status of his dynasty by marrying a princess of Palenque. He also built a new temple-pyramid that featured a remarkable stairway: 72 steps, each 50 feet wide, inscribed with a total of more than 1,250 glyphs that told the story of Copán and its rulers. The stairway was the longest written inscription in all of the Americas. Sadly, it collapsed in the 18th century, and now only a few of the glyphs remain in their original order. The epigraphers—specialists in writing and inscriptions—who have worked to sort the broken pieces of the symbols and put them back in order have compared the task to the world's largest jigsaw puzzle.

The last king of the Blue-Quetzal-Macaw dynasty was Yax-Pac, who came to the throne in 763. Although he erected a number of monuments and altars that portray him as a mighty ruler, Copán was already in decline. The combination of population growth and poor harvests led to food shortages that weakened the people; scientists have analyzed skeletons from the site, and their findings suggest that as much as 90 percent of Copán's later population suffered from malnutrition and disease. Yax-Pac died in 820, and the days of Copán's royal glory ended. Archaeologists have found evidence that people continued to live in the valley for the next three or four hundred years, but their numbers steadily diminished, and nothing new was built. By about 1200, Copán was uninhabited except for a few farmers and hunters, and the forest began its slow, patient work of reclaiming the valley and covering the monuments.

Copán's decline mirrored the decline of Classic Maya civilization in general. Tikal, Palenque, and other centers in the southern lowlands all seem to have been abandoned sometime around the 10th century. To the north, in Yucatán, Maya culture continued to flourish at such cities as Chichén Itzá, Uxmal, Tulum, and Mayapan, but these communities were well past their prime by the 15th century. When the Spanish arrived in the 16th century, the Maya were in disarray, their cultural peak already several centuries in the past. The ancient Maya believed in a cycle of time that called for the world to end in A.D. 2012. The world of Maya glory ended centuries ahead of schedule.

Historians still do not know what caused the end of Maya civilization, a decline that archaeologist Robert L. Sharer of the University of Pennsylvania has called "one of the most profound cultural failures in human history." Most researchers feel that warfare among the Maya cities and rivalry among nobles within the cities, together with economic and environmental problems resulting from drought, deforestation, and overpopulation, led to a general breakdown of order. Under the stress of prolonged warfare, diminishing crop yields, and perhaps unrest among the peasants, the highly structured, rigidly governed Maya societies simply fell apart.

Researchers are still filling in the picture of the Maya collapse. In 1995, for example, geologists found evidence that the decline of Maya cities in the southern Yucatán in the 8th century coincided with the worst drought that area had experienced in more than 7,000 years. According to Jeremy Sabloff, director of the University of Pennsylvania Museum of Archaeology and Anthropology, the drought was one of "a whole series of strains" that caused the Maya to abandon

Tulum and other nearby cities soon after they had reached their prime. Scholars agree that why and how the Maya culture collapsed are among the most absorbing questions in Maya studies today.

We have learned what we know about the Maya from three sources. Historians have combed archives in many countries for chronicles—often long-forgotten and covered with dust—by Diego de Landa and other Europeans who witnessed the final years of the Maya culture. Archaeologists have excavated the temples and pyramids at Copán and other sites; they have also studied the ruins of peasant villages, road systems, agricultural canals, and fields for clues about the Mayas' social and political lives and their economy. And epigraphers have struggled to decipher the texts and inscriptions of the Maya—the only written language developed by a native culture in the Americas.

Deciphering these texts is an enormous challenge. The Maya may have left behind thousands of books, or codices, but only four of these survived the wrath of the Spanish missionaries and the ravages of time. Nearly all of the Maya writing that remained consisted of glyphs, or symbols, painted on pottery or carved in stone on stelae, doorways, and other architectural features. Gazing at these mysterious symbols, John Lloyd Stephens asked, "Who shall read them?" Stephens believed that someone, someday, would decipher the lost Maya script.

The first epigraphers to study the Maya script approached the glyphs as pictographs, or picture writing, in which each glyph represented an object, concept, or number. Scholars first managed to decipher the Maya number system. The results were impressive: The Maya were accomplished mathematicians whose number system included the zero centuries before Arab mathematicians discovered this useful mathematical tool. Skilled astronomers and timekeepers, the Maya believed that time repeated itself in cycles.

Decoding the Mayan glyphs was one of the most significant achievements of modern scholars. Breakthroughs in reading the glyphs since the 1950s have given us a whole new view of the Maya and their culture.

They developed elaborate, interlocking calendars to measure the solar year of the seasons and the sacred year of the gods.

By the middle of the 20th century, researchers had developed an image of the Maya as a philosophical race of mathematicians, astronomers, and priests, interested chiefly in measuring the passage of time and watching the stars. Many archaeologists believed that all of the still-undeciphered Maya glyphs had to do with calendars, astronomy, and religion.

A revolution in Maya epigraphy began in the 1950s, when Russian scholar Yuri Knorosov took a bold new approach to studying the glyphs: He suggested that the Maya script—like that of ancient Egypt and China—combined picture writing with phonetic writing. In other words, the glyphs could represent sounds as well as whole words or ideas. Knorosov's breakthrough allowed epigraphers to begin the painstaking task of matching glyphs to sounds. They used information about the sounds of Maya words recorded by Landa in his 16th-century chronicle, which had been rediscovered in the mid-19th century.

Found at Copán, this Mayan sculpture from around A.D. 770 represents the god of maize, or corn.

Tatiana Proskouriakoff, a Russian-born scholar who worked in the United States, made the next breakthrough in 1960. As she studied the dates in Maya glyphs, she realized that many inscriptions contained sets of dates 56 to 64 years apart—the average length of a human lifespan in Maya times. Proskouriakoff concluded that Maya texts dealt not with religion but with history: with events such as royal births, reigns, wars, and deaths. For the first time, the Maya script was understood to tell the stories of actual men and women. The history of the ancient Maya suddenly became specific. Rulers and their families acquired names, birthdates, and detailed life stories.

Since the breakthroughs made by Knorosov and Proskouriakoff, scholars have deciphered more than 80 percent of all known Maya glyphs. They have created a new picture of Maya culture and society. We now know that the world of the ancient Maya was not a single, unified empire, but rather a patchwork of rival kingdoms or city-states that warred with one another more often than they made diplomatic alliances. These aggressive, competitive kingdoms shared a common religion. In the Maya view of the cosmos, the human world was poised precariously between an underworld of demons and an overworld of gods. People were at the mercy of sudden destructive forces; to keep those forces at bay they engaged in solemn rituals, sometimes including animal or human sacrifice. Prisoners of war were sacrificed both for religious reasons and to demonstrate the power of the victor. One of the most important Maya religious rituals was bloodletting, in which worshippers offered up their own blood—often in very painful ways—to satisfy the gods and keep the universe in its proper order. Some sculptures show kings and queens performing the bloodlettings on themselves.

Copán, the first of the "cities buried in forests" that Stephens and Catherwood saw, has contributed a great deal to our knowledge of the Maya. Copán's many stelae and other inscriptions were a rich source of material for the epigraphers who finally succeeded in deciphering the Maya script, opening up the Maya records of politics and history. And although exploration and excavation have been going on at Copán for a century, important discoveries are still being made. In 1989, a team of Honduran and American archaeologists uncovered the first royal tomb ever found at Copán. Hidden under one of the stairways on the main pyramid, the tomb contained the body of a middle-aged man, along with the largest collection of jade ornaments and earrings ever found at Copán. Pots of paint and other clues found in the tomb suggest that the man was a royal scribe, possibly a younger son of the king Smoke-Jaguar. In 1992 a team from the University of Pennsylvania found another tomb buried in the heart of the pyramid. This one appears to contain the body of one of Copán's 6th-century kings.

In 1982, Copán was declared a World Heritage site by the United Nations Scientific, Educational, and Cultural Organization; this made U.N. funds available to protect the site from looting and decay and to pay for research projects. Two years later, the Honduran government made Copán a national archaeological park, and work began on an archaeological museum there, scheduled to open in 1996. While much of Copán has been excavated, field archaeologists and epigraphers will be working on the site for decades to come. Long after Stephens and Catherwood first marveled at its mysteries, Copán remains enigmatic, many of its secrets still untouched.

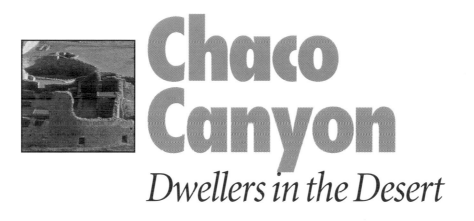

CHAPTER 5

Chaco Canyon
Dwellers in the Desert

*T*he United States government had two goals in northwestern New Mexico in the late 1840s. Its first goal was to subdue the Navajo Indians, who were resisting white settlement in their tribal territories. Second, government officials wanted to find and map a good route across the rugged landscape for the use of soldiers, settlers, and, eventually, railroad builders.

To bring the Navajo under control, the U.S. Army sent out a colonel and a detachment of troops from Santa Fe in the summer of 1849. To carry out the route-finding mission, the Army assigned Lieutenant James Hervey Simpson to accompany the troops. Simpson was a member of the Army's Corps of Topographical Engineers, an elite group of surveyors and mapmakers who played a leading role in the exploration of the American West. Along with Simpson went two brothers named Richard and Ned Kern. The Kerns were artists; their job was to help Simpson illustrate and map his findings.

The expedition marched northwest from Santa Fe, tracked the Navajo to their hideout in a canyon along

Pueblo Bonito in Chaco Canyon (background), where this pottery pitcher was found. Chaco Canyon was once a center of the Native American Anasazi culture.

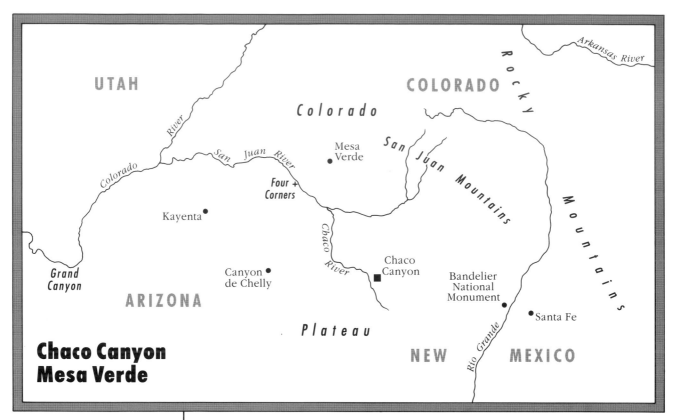

**Chaco Canyon
Mesa Verde**

the Chaco River, and defeated them. A few days later the soldiers marched west into what is now northeastern Arizona, to another Navajo stronghold called Canyon de Chelly. Again the army won a victory over the Navajo. But Simpson and the Kerns were more interested in their surroundings than in these skirmishes. In Chaco Canyon and Canyon de Chelly they had found huge buildings of weathered reddish stone that seemed to grow right out of the valley floors and walls. In the course of a military expedition, they had made one of the greatest archaeological discoveries of a century filled with marvelous finds. They had come upon the ancient dwelling places of a Native American people known to modern archaeologists as the Anasazi.

The ruins were unlike anything Lieutenant Simpson had ever seen. Chaco Canyon, in particular, was an astonishing discovery. Along a 10-mile stretch of this canyon, gouged out of a barren sandstone plateau by the Chaco River, stood the remains of a string of pueblos, or villages. Some of the large pueblos stood on the valley floor; others perched on the rim of the canyon, high above the floor. Each pueblo was a single, sprawling, freestanding structure, flat-roofed and multistoried, with dozens, in some cases hundreds, of rooms.

Simpson and the Kerns spent several days measuring, mapping, and sketching the ruins. Simpson was particularly struck by the fine stonework of the ruins, which were made of many small brick-shaped stones tidily fitted together like "a magnificent piece of mosaic work." Later scientists were to discover that just one of the Chaco Canyon pueblos, Chetro Ketl, contained 50 million pieces of cut and shaped sandstone; it was probably built in stages over more than a century.

Simpson prepared a report on his journey for his superiors in Washington, D.C. Although his principal subject was the route-finding and surveying he had done, he also described the ruins. A version of the report was published in 1852 and awakened some interest in Chaco Canyon. In the decades that followed, the surveyors, prospectors, and other travelers who swarmed into the Southwest found similar sites scattered throughout the region that is now called Four Corners, where the states of Utah, Colorado, New Mexico, and Arizona meet. Some of these ruins were freestanding pueblos like those in Chaco Canyon. Others were cliff dwellings, stacked atop one another under overhanging canyon rims or built into natural or human-made caves. They ranged in size from one or two rooms to huge complexes that looked as though they had once housed hundreds of people.

In 1874, frontier photographer William Henry Jackson was traveling through southwestern Colorado when he heard stories of remarkable ruins nearby, at a place called Mesa Verde. Jackson visited Mesa Verde and photographed a two-story dwelling on a ledge partway up the 800-foot cliff that forms the wall of the mesa. Jackson's photographs were shown at the Centennial Exposition in Philadelphia in 1876 and were a huge success. At the time no one knew that Jackson had missed the even more spectacular cliff dwellings just a short distance away in a side canyon.

One of the most enthusiastic explorers of the Southwest was Adolph Bandelier, a middle-aged Illinois banker who yearned to see breathtaking landscapes and study ancient cultures. In 1880, Bandelier received a grant from the Archaeological Institute of America, then a brand-new organization. With the

"Pothunters" sift the dirt of Chaco Canyon in 1896, looking for turquoise beads. The U.S. government soon closed the Chaco Canyon site to amateur excavators, who had stripped thousands of artifacts from the ruins.

AIA's money, Bandelier went to Santa Fe, New Mexico, bought a mule, and began his travels. He crisscrossed New Mexico for 18 months before heading off to South America, where he spent more than a decade. Of the 167 ruins that Bandelier saw in New Mexico, the most dramatic was shown to him by Juan Jose Montoya, his Native American guide. Montoya led Bandelier to a canyon called Rito de Frijoles (Bean Creek), across the Rio Grande from Santa Fe. There Bandelier saw a long row of crumbling dwellings at the foot of an immense cliff. Behind the dwellings were caves, some natural and some human-made, that clearly had formed part of the abandoned city. Today the Rito de Frijoles site is called Bandelier National Monument in honor of Adolph Bandelier, who called the place "the grandest thing I ever saw."

The next discoverer was as eager to exploit the ruins of the Southwest as to explore them. He was a Colorado rancher named Richard Wetherill. In 1888, while tracking cattle in a snowstorm on top of the high tableland called Mesa Verde, Wetherill came to the edge of a steep canyon he had not seen before. Peering out and down through the whirling flakes, Wetherill saw an astounding sight. Half a mile away, on the far side of the steep sandstone canyon, was a silent, empty city of stacked cliff houses: the extensive ruins that William Henry Jackson had missed on his visit to Mesa Verde 14 years before. Before the day was out, Wetherill and his brother-in-law had climbed down into the canyon and made their way up into the cliff city. They wandered from room to room, picking up artifacts that had lain undisturbed—and probably unobserved—for 600 years.

Wetherill and his family viewed the ruins as a money-making opportunity. They spent the winter collecting artifacts from the ruins and sold the collection in Denver for $3000 the following spring. By 1893, the Wetherills had sold four collections of pottery, turquoise jewelry, tools, and even mummies from the ru-

Colorado rancher Richard Wetherill came across the cliff city city at Mesa Verde in 1888 while on a cattle drive. He and his family (his wife is seen here, third from right) combined genuine interest in the vanished Anasazi with the desire to cash in on their relics.

ins. Today such pothunting—the random collecting of artifacts from archaeological sites—is rightly condemned as unscientific and insensitive to the cultural traditions of Native Americans. It is also illegal. In Wetherill's time, however, it was common, and many museums acquired prized items from pothunters.

To Wetherill's credit, he *did* request scientific guidance from both the Smithsonian Institution and Harvard University's Peabody Museum. Both turned him down. The only scientific help Wetherill received in his early years

A room in Pueblo Bonito. Archaeologists estimate that the pueblo once had 800 or more such chambers.

of pothunting came from a young Swedish scholar who visited him in 1891 and introduced him to the idea of stratigraphy—the relationship between the layers of earth and the age of artifacts. Despite his commercial approach to artifacts, Wetherill seems to have had a genuine interest in the ruins and their builders. Some of the theories that he advanced about these long-vanished Indians have been upheld by later scholars. It was Wetherill who gave the name "Anasazi," a Navajo word that means "ancient ones," to the unknown builders of the cliff city at Mesa Verde and other, similar ruins in the Four Corners area. Today, recognizing that a Navajo name makes little sense for a people who had no relation to the Navajo, the Park Service has begun calling the Anasazi the Ancient Pueblan Peoples.

In 1895, Wetherill turned his attention to Chaco Canyon. By now he had acquired two backers: a wealthy New York family of soap manufacturers and the American Museum of Natural History. They sponsored an expedition that began excavating Pueblo Bonito, one of the best-preserved buildings in Chaco Canyon, in 1896. The diggers uncovered dozens of pottery bowls and thousands of pieces of turquoise, and then they came upon several burial chambers filled with arrows, jewelry, and other items. At the end of the season, they shipped a freight car full of Anasazi artifacts to the Museum of Natural History.

Four years later, Wetherill and his colleagues had stripped 190 of Pueblo Bonito's surviving rooms of their relics. Scientists and government officials, worried that the unregulated activities of amateurs like Wetherill were spoiling irreplaceable archaeological sites, shut down Wetherill's dig in 1900. Yet pothunters still flocked to the site to grub for pots and other artifacts, which brought high prices from private collectors and museums in the United States and Europe. In 1907, the federal government made Chaco Canyon a national monument. Since that time work at the site has been carried out by authorized expeditions. As for Wetherill, he came to an inglorious end in 1910, shot to death in a fight over a stolen horse. He was buried in an Anasazi burial site at Pueblo Bonito.

Archaeologists call the early Anasazi the Basket Makers because they wove baskets and fiber pouches. This one was used to store corn.

In the years since Lieutenant Simpson first gaped in amazement at the Chaco Canyon pueblos, we have learned a great deal about the people Wetherill dubbed the Anasazi. Archaeologists now know that the Anasazi culture arose in the rugged, high-desert tablelands of the Four Corners region around A.D. 200. The early Anasazi lived in pit houses, shallow depressions in the earth that were lined with flat stones, walled with logs, and roofed with poles. Scholars call these early Anasazi the Basket Makers because they wove extremely strong and useful baskets for food storage. They wore sandals, belts, and aprons of woven plant fiber, with hide cloaks and rabbit-fur blankets in the winter.

Around A.D. 600, the Basket Maker phase gave way to the Pueblo phase of Anasazi culture. The people of this era mastered the art of making pottery, and eventually they developed a distinctive Anasazi style of pottery that used white clay, which was painted with human or animal figures or complex geometric patterns in black. At this time, too, the Anasazi began moving out of their pit houses and into surface structures of stone and adobe, or baked mud brick. But these new communities included underground chambers similar to the old pit houses. The chambers do not seem to have been used as living quarters; most scientists call them *kivas,* the name used today by Indians of the Southwest for underground chambers where religious ceremonies and gatherings of tribal societies take place. Each Anasazi village had at least one kiva, which was entered by a ladder. Anthropologists believe that to the Anasazi, the kiva was a place of connection between the world of the living and the world of the spirits, especially the spirits of ancestors.

By about A.D. 1000, the Anasazi culture was entering its most impressive phase, the Great House period, during which the enormous cliff and canyon pueblos were built. By this time the Anasazi had established tens of thousands of sites in more than 25,000 square miles of the Four Corners area—modern archaeologists have identified 22,000 sites in New Mexico alone. There were three main branches of Anasazi settlement: the Mesa Verde region in Colorado, the Kayenta region in northeastern Arizona, and the Chaco Canyon region in New Mexico. Of these, Chaco Canyon was the most elaborate. Much of what we know about the Anasazi has been learned at Chaco Canyon, which is not only the largest Anasazi site, but also the largest cluster of archaeological remains in the United States.

Chaco Canyon has 13 Great Houses, or large pueblos, of which Pueblo Bonito is the largest. Each pueblo contains a number of kivas; Pueblo Bonito alone has 32 of these ceremonial chambers. The canyon also has at least 2,400 smaller sites, ranging from traces of hunters' campfires thousands of years old to the more recent artifacts, such as outlying Anasazi buildings or cave dwellings.

Pueblo Bonito was probably built over a span of about 200 years. The pueblo was partially crumbled when Simpson saw it in 1849, but from what remained standing archaeologists have been able to picture what it looked like in its prime. Four stories tall in places, it contained at least 800 rooms arranged in a sweeping semicircle, with the sacred kivas in the center. The rooms were quite similar to one another; most measured about 13 by 16 feet. Rooms on the upper levels were entered by pole ladders or by holes in their roofs. The flat roofs were used as plazas, as work areas for spinning wool and weaving, or for drying and storing food. The inhabitants used little furniture—only one wooden stool has been found in the entire pueblo, although some of the rooms had built-in stone benches or storage cupboards along the walls. People probably slept on mats of woven plants or on blankets. Large storage chambers in the lower levels held a communal food supply. Wooden beams supported the floors and roofs of the pueblos. Each room required about 40 beams, and each beam came from a single fir or

pine tree. Scientists have estimated that nearly a quarter of a million trees were used in building the pueblos of Chaco Canyon. Enormous effort and cooperation must have been needed to obtain the beams, for they came from a forest about 40 miles away. Many of these wooden beams have survived the centuries, preserved by the dry air of Chaco Canyon.

The wooden beams of Pueblo Bonito helped modern researchers solve the pressing problem of dating the ruins. At the beginning of the 20th century, archaeologists were asking, "How old are these pueblos?" The answer came from the unexpected combination of astronomy and trees. Andrew E. Douglass, an astronomer at the University of Arizona, was interested in sunspots, events that occur on the sun in 11-year cycles. He wondered whether the sunspots affected the earth's weather. One way to find out, he speculated, was to examine the growth rings of living trees. It was well known that a ring forms in a tree's wood for each year of the tree's growth, and that the rings reflect certain weather conditions. Broad rings correspond to years of heavy rain and much growth; thin rings to years of light rain and less growth. Douglass thought that the growth rings from living Arizona trees, reflecting the region's rainfall history, might show 11-year cycles corresponding to sunspots.

As Douglass worked with samples from older and older trees, he gradually built up a "chronology" of tree growth rings for the past several hundred years. In 1923, he began examining the growth rings in wooden beams at Pueblo Bonito. By patiently comparing growth-ring patterns and linking recent samples to

The Anasazi used natural caves and also dug new ones in the soft sandstone walls of their canyons. With the ladders pulled up, the cave dwellings were safe from attack.

older ones when their patterns overlapped, Douglass eventually extended his record of matching rings nearly 2,000 years into the past. Douglass had created the science of dendrochronology, the use of tree rings to date archaeological structures and sites. Using Douglass's chronology, scientists can tell, for example, that a particular beam at Pueblo Bonito came from a tree that started growing in 1237 and was chopped down in 1380. Dendrochronology has proved particularly helpful to archaeologists working in the Southwest, where the dry climate preserves wood well.

An offshoot of dendrochronology is dendroclimatology, the study of the relationship between climate and trees. Dendroclimatology allows scientists to track climate and weather changes over time by examining tree rings. In addition, just as at Petra, vegetation sealed in old pack-rat middens in the Southwest yields much information about climate conditions in bygone times. From tree rings and pack-rat middens, researchers have built up a picture of the Four Corners climate during the centuries when the Anasazi flourished.

One of the most striking features of Chaco Canyon, as of most Anasazi settlements, is the inhospitable nature of the land: cold in winter, hot in summer, arid most of the time. To flourish in such an environment, the Anasazi had to make the most of every resource. They harnessed the irregular rainfall and the unreliable river by building cisterns for water storage and simple stone dams to divert rainfall into them. They made ditches to irrigate their fields of corn, beans, and squash, the basic elements of their diet, supplemented by deer, antelope, rabbit, and mountain sheep brought in by the hunters. Still, conditions were marginal. Tree rings in the pueblos' roof beams show that Chaco Canyon experienced many dry years, during which the community had to rely on stored food reserves and on food imported from other communities.

Researchers at Chaco, impressed by the size of the pueblos, used to call the pueblos "prehistoric apartment buildings" and estimated the canyon's population at 10,000 or even higher. But as archaeologists continued to study the canyon, they became aware of some inconsistencies. The food, water, and firewood resources of the area were simply not sufficient for a permanent population of that size. Furthermore, many of the rooms in the pueblos did not look as though

they had been occupied over long periods of time. Some experts now believe that the pueblos of Chaco were ceremonial centers, not true cities. The canyon's full-time population probably numbered just a few thousand, but periodically Anasazi from all over the area gathered in the pueblos for large assemblies that may have combined religious ceremonies with trade fairs.

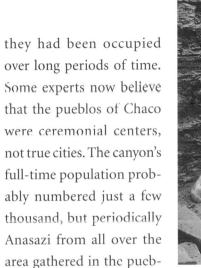

Pottery recovered from Pueblo Bonito. Around A.D. 600, the Anasazi turned from making baskets to making pottery.

These ritual gatherings were probably connected with the seasons. The Anasazi were keen observers of the sun and the stars, whose apparent movements and changing positions in the sky regulated such important activities as planting and harvesting. Certain features of Anasazi architecture reflect astronomical knowledge. For example, the entrance to the great kiva at Casa Rinconada, one of the Chaco pueblos, faces the point in the northern sky around which the stars appear to revolve. Windows in several of the pueblos seem to act as solar calendars—at key dates in the solar years, such as the summer and winter solstices (the longest and shortest days), the light shines directly through these windows.

One clue to the possible ceremonial or ritual significance of Chaco Canyon is the network of prehistoric paths that converge on the canyon. Almost invisible from the ground, these ancient roadways were discovered by 20th-century pilots and mapped by high-technology satellite photography. The pathways radiate out from the canyon in many directions. Unlike most Indian trails, they are perfectly straight and do not circle hills or other obstructions. Some anthropologists believe that these paths were sacred highways, constructed as religious symbols or for use in ceremonies. The roadways probably had more utilitarian uses as well, serving as routes for trade and communication.

The ruins of Pueblo Bonito. The round chambers are much like the kivas used today by Native Americans of the Southwest for religious ceremonies and gatherings of tribal leaders.

Some of the artifacts found in Chaco Canyon show that the Anasazi who lived there were part of a far-reaching Indian trade network. They traded with other Anasazi communities, as shown by the presence of pottery from Mesa Verde in the Chaco Canyon pueblos. The people of Chaco Canyon also traded for goods from farther away: Archaeologists have found seashells from the Pacific coast and parrot feathers and copper bells from Mexico among the ruins. The Chacoans may have paid for these goods with turquoise beads. Hoards of such beads, totalling half a million, have been found in the pueblos.

Because the Anasazi left no written records, we may never know for certain why they abandoned the huge cliff and pueblo dwellings that had cost them so much labor. There is little evidence of war or plague, but the tree rings at Chaco Canyon tell the story of a period of good rainfall followed by a long drought. From 1050 until 1130, Chaco Canyon experienced year after year of generous rains. Then the dry years began. A series of prolonged droughts in the 12th and 13th centuries must have made it increasingly difficult for people to survive in the canyon. By about 1200, the Chacoans had cut down all the trees in the area;

Each Anasazi group developed distinctive pottery designs based on triangles, squares, or other shapes. By tracking the different pottery styles at each site, archaeologists can trace patterns of trade among Anasazi communities.

this deforestation not only caused their precious farmland to erode, but may have helped cause the droughts.

Water and food shortages put too great a strain on the large pueblos. By 1300, the pueblos of Chaco Canyon were empty. Researchers today believe that the inhabitants dispersed from the pueblos to live in smaller family or clan settlements elsewhere in the Four Corners area. Some of the Chacoans may have migrated to Rito de Frijoles; archaeologists working at Bandelier National Monument have determined that the pueblos there were occupied for a century or more after Chaco Canyon was abandoned, probably because that area had a slightly wetter climate and volcanic soil that retained moisture. Archaeologists have also discovered that the people who lived in the area of present-day Bandelier were closely linked to the Chacoan culture.

Chaco Canyon was not the only Anasazi community to disperse under the stress of food and water shortages. The entire Four Corners region experienced long droughts. The fragile soil in most Anasazi communities could no longer produce the crops needed to sustain large settlements. Mesa Verde and nearly all other Anasazi settlements were emptied at about the same time the Chacoans abandoned their pueblos. Although the Anasazi moved away from their "Great Houses," they did not simply vanish. They migrated south to the Rio Grande valley, where their descendants, the Zuni and Hopi, live today. In their architecture, their traditional farming practices, and their spiritual beliefs, these contemporary Native Americans have kept many elements of Anasazi culture alive.

CHAPTER 6

Angkor
The Butterfly Hunter's Find

Henri Mouhot loved to travel. Born in France in 1826, he went to Russia when he was only 18 and stayed for 10 years, teaching French, seeing as much of the country as he could manage, and training himself in the new art of photography. He then spent two years traveling with his brother in western Europe, after which the two Mouhots married English women and settled on Jersey, an island in the channel between England and France.

On Jersey, Henri Mouhot devoted himself to the study of natural history—a catchall term for zoology, botany, and geology—and read books about faraway places. These studies awakened his wanderlust, and he decided to travel again. Just then he happened to read a book about the country of Siam in Southeast Asia. (Siam is now known as Thailand.) At once Mouhot made up his mind to visit Southeast Asia, and by October 1858 he had arrived in Bangkok, the capital of Siam. He would spend the next three years exploring and collecting plant and

People who lived near the ruins of Angkor (background) claimed that the city had been built by a legendary leper king, represented in the statue at right.

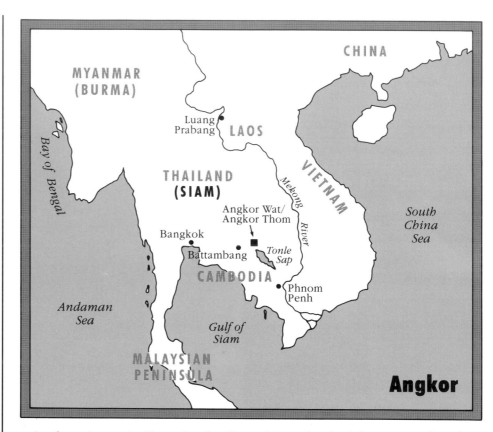

Angkor

animal specimens in Siam, Cambodia, and Laos, but he is best remembered to-day for three weeks in January 1860.

At the time, Mouhot was at a town called Battambang in Cambodia's thickly forested, low-lying central plain. He had heard that there were stone ruins off to the east, across a huge lake called the Tonle Sap. With the help of a Roman Catholic priest from a nearby French missionary outpost, Mouhot boated across the Tonle Sap. The route then led, Mouhot reported, along "a dusty sandy path passing through a dense forest of stunted trees." Mouhot followed his guide through this rather gloomy landscape for some time. On either side of the path were rocks and low hills covered with moss, vines, and full-grown trees.

Then Mouhot saw ahead of him a long platform of rock, with a staircase leading up to it. Suddenly he realized that the rocky outcroppings he had taken for jungle-covered hillocks were really buildings and statues of carved stone, cracked into pieces by tree roots. He had been walking among ruins for some time. He climbed the stone steps and found himself on a raised road or causeway paved with huge blocks of stone. It crossed a wide moat. At the far end of the causeway a cluster of tall, tapering towers rose above a long columned wall, and even from a distance Mouhot could see that the crumbling towers were covered with sculptured ornamentation. To Mouhot, the ruins in the midst of the dense jungle were a striking sight, "which presents itself to the eye of the traveller, making him forget all the fatigues of his journey, filling him with admiration and delight, such as would be experienced on finding a verdant oasis in the sandy desert." Mouhot had arrived at a place called Angkor, which means "the center" or "the capital" in the Khmer language of Cambodia. The building upon which he gazed with such delight was a temple called Angkor Wat.

Mouhot spent three weeks exploring and sketching Angkor Wat and some of the other vine-covered ruins nearby, including Angkor Thom, a walled palace. He was impressed by the sheer size of the ruins. Of Angkor Wat, he wrote:

> What strikes the observer with not less admiration than the grandeur, regularity, and beauty of these majestic buildings, is the immense size and prodigious number of the blocks of stone of which they are constructed. In this temple alone are as many as 1532 columns. What means of transport, what a multitude of workmen, must this have required, seeing that the mountain out of which the stone was hewn is thirty miles distant!

The stones, he noted, had once fitted together perfectly without mortar—although many of them had been forced apart or toppled by vines and the intrusive roots of trees, which over time can wrench even huge stones from their places.

Like many later visitors, Mouhot was haunted by the desolation of the site, which gave rise to melancholy musings:

> All this region is now as lonely and deserted as formerly it must have been full of life and cheerfulness; and the howling of wild animals, and the cries of a few birds, alone disturb the solitude.
>
> Sad fragility of human things! How many centuries and thousands of generations have passed away, of which history, probably, will never tell us anything: what riches and treasures of art will remain for ever buried beneath

Henri Mouhot called
the world's attention
to Angkor. Mouhot's
brother called him
"the intrepid traveller,
whom death carried
off . . . in the midst of
his discoveries."

these ruins; how many distinguished men—artists, sovereigns, and warriors—whose names were worthy of immortality, are now forgotten, laid to rest under the thick dust which covers these tombs!

Mouhot left Angkor and continued on his way, gathering insects, especially butterflies. He hoped that his collection would make a significant contribution to natural history. Sadly, Mouhot the naturalist was doomed to disappointment. He shipped his precious specimens home but later received word that the ship on which they had been sent had sunk. "And so all my poor insects, which have cost me so much care and pains for so many months, are lost for ever—some of them rare and valuable specimens, which, alas! I shall probably never be able to replace," he mourned in his journal.

Undaunted, Mouhot rested for a while in Bangkok and then set out to explore the Mekong River in Laos, where he expected to obtain new and better insect specimens. Not far from Luang Prabang, the capital of Laos, Mouhot fell ill with a tropical fever. He died on November 10, 1861. His servants buried him and carried his papers and specimens back to Bangkok. From there Mouhot's belongings were shipped to his brother, who published Mouhot's journal in French in 1863; an English version followed in 1864.

Henri Mouhot was not the first outsider to look upon Angkor. Indeed, as historian Michael Smithies points out in his introduction to the 1989 edition of Mouhot's journals, Angkor was "a good deal less lost than popular legend has it." As early as 1550, a Portuguese historian mentioned Angkor in an account of Cambodia that was part of Portugal's colonial archives. Angkor was also mentioned in several Spanish books published during the 16th and 17th centuries, when Spain was colonizing parts of Asia. In 1819, a French scholar published a translation of a description of Angkor that had been written in the 13th century by Zhou Daguan, a Chinese diplomat who spent time there. Several other references to the ruins appeared in the European press during the 1850s.

Even if Mouhot did not discover Angkor, he did more than anyone else to stimulate interest in it. His book not only contained the most detailed description of Angkor yet written, but also included a number of splendid illustrations of the ruins made from his sketches. Mouhot's account was far more widely read than the earlier ones, and it prompted a stream of European and American travelers to visit the ruins.

All of these visitors had one question: Who built Angkor? Mouhot wrote that a traveler coming upon the ruins "cannot but ask what has become of this powerful race, so civilised, so enlightened, the authors of these gigantic works?" One of the 17th-century Spanish chroniclers had suggested that Angkor had been built by Alexander the Great or by the Roman emperor Trajan—although neither Greek nor Roman history records such an event.

Mouhot thought that some aspects of the ruins looked rather Egyptian. He did not think that the ruins had been built by the Khmers, as the people of Cambodia are called. Neither did the Khmers he met. Whenever Mouhot asked a Khmer about the origin of Angkor, he was told that it had been built by giants, or by gods, or by a legendary leper king, or that it had built itself.

A pavilion inside Angkor Wat, drawn from one of Mouhot's sketches.

The systematic study of Angkor began in 1898, when the French—who had made Cambodia into a French protectorate—set up a research organization to oversee work at the ruins. Most of the researchers' efforts were aimed not at traditional archaeology but at preservation. If archaeologists were ever to unlock the secrets of Angkor, they had to keep Angkor from disappearing.

Unlike desert ruins, which may remain unchanged for centuries in a dry, barren climate, the ruins at Angkor were being eroded by rain and ripped apart by the encroaching jungle. As Pierre Loti, a French naval officer and writer who visited the site at around this time, put it, "The fig tree is the ruler of Angkor today. Over the palaces and over the temples which it had patiently pried apart, everywhere it unfolds its smooth pale branches, and its dome of foliage." The conservators began experimenting with ways of cleaning and shoring up the crumbling temples and palaces. They started by hacking away the vegetation that had swallowed up all but the tallest rooftops and filled all of the rooms and passageways.

At the same time, archaeologists were studying the sculptures and inscriptions on the walls of Angkor. Gradually the history of the place emerged from the cloudy realms of myth and fantasy. Despite a few far-fetched theories that linked Angkor with the Mayan ruins in Central America, it soon became clear that the builders of Angkor were none other than the Khmers, the ancestors of the modern inhabitants of Cambodia. Angkor, it turned out, was the creation of a mighty Khmer civilization.

The rise of the Khmer people dated from about the 1st century A.D., when a kingdom called Funan arose in what is now Cambodia. Funan was a power in Southeast Asia until 550. Many features of Funanese culture were borrowed from India, with which Funan developed close trading ties. In particular, the Indian religions of Hinduism and Buddhism took root in Funan. The Funanese built brick temples with layered, tapering roofs, a style similar to Indian religious architecture.

The Khmer people lived in the northern part of Funan, in a state called Zhenla. In the 6th century, Zhenla overthrew Funan, and the Khmer became the rulers of a state they called Kambuja (Cambodia is the modern form of this name). Like the Funanese, the Khmers had many links with India. They used the Sanskrit language of India, they worshiped Hindu gods, and they built temples that reached skyward with towers that, like those on Indian temples, symbolized mountains sacred to Siva, the Hindu god who represents the forces of creation and destruction in the universe.

In the early 9th century, a powerful Khmer king named Jayavarman II unified the fragmented states of the region into a Khmer empire that dominated Southeast Asia for several centuries. Temples and other ruins dating from his reign are found near Angkor, but it was not until the reign of Yasovarman I (889–900) that Angkor became the Khmer capital. The golden age of Angkor was the 11th and 12th centuries. King Suryavarman I (reigned 1011–1050) built the imperial palace of Angkor Thom. A century later, Suryavarman II (reigned

1113–1150) built Angkor Wat, the largest and most magnificent of the Khmer temples.

The last of the great Khmer builder-kings was Jayavarman VII (reigned 1181–1220). He rebuilt much of Angkor Thom, adding a moat around the palace. Jayavarman VII also built three large temple complexes outside the city walls and hundreds of temples, monasteries, hospitals, and wayfarers' lodges throughout Kambuja. His most impressive achievement, however, was the construction of Angkor's second-largest temple, the Bayon, which stands at the center of Angkor Thom.

By the time of Jayavarman VII, Buddhism had replaced Hinduism as the religion of the Khmer rulers. The Bayon was built as a Buddhist temple. At about the same time, many of the earlier Hindu temples were made into Buddhist shrines. For this reason, Angkor's sculptures and statues reflect both Hinduism and Buddhism. For example, a series of large wall carvings at Angkor Wat represents an episode from Hindu mythology— the god Vishnu churning the "milky ocean" of the universe to create the earth, as a person churns milk to make butter. But the Bayon, built a generation later, is adorned with the Buddha's image.

Before archaeologists could begin studying Angkor, they had to protect it from further destruction by jungle plants, which were slowly tearing the buildings apart.

The expense of constructing Angkor's palaces and temples, together with the cost of constant military campaigns against rival states to the east, north, and west, may have weakened the Khmer empire. Kambuja entered a period of decline. In 1431, the Thai king-

A procession of gods from a wall carving in the Bayon, Angkor's second-largest temple, which stands at the center of Angkor Thom.

dom west of Kambuja captured the western Khmer provinces, including Angkor. The Khmers fled Angkor, taking most of its treasure with them, and established a new capital 150 miles away at Phnom Penh, which remains the capital of Cambodia today. The victorious Thai looted whatever precious items remained at Angkor and then left the area.

Years passed. Rain washed the faces of Angkor's statues; seeds in bird droppings took root on its roofs and walls. Gradually Angkor was overgrown and forgotten.

Then Mouhot's visit awakened interest in the site and the French established themselves as its caretakers. In clearing away the jungle so that they could accurately assess the site, they discovered that Angkor is much more extensive than Mouhot dreamed.

The Angkor ruins cover a district of 124 square miles. Within this district are several hundred monuments; some are small shrines, others immense temples and palaces. The design of most of these structures is based upon a symbol that had great importance to the Khmer people: the mandala.

The mandala is a feature of both the Hindu and the Buddhist religions and often appears in Asian wall hangings or sacred paintings. It is a cosmological symbol—that is, it reflects a cosmology, or belief about the way the universe is organized. There are hundreds of different mandalas, but all represent a sacred landscape. The center of the landscape is usually a square with four gates or doorways; at the center of the square is the image of a Buddha, another deity, or a holy mountain. The mountain is Mount Meru, a holy place believed by both Hindus and Buddhists to be the center of the earth.

Like many temples in India and elsewhere in Asia, the Khmer holy buildings at Angkor were built in the form of three-dimensional mandalas. They are enclosed in square courtyards with four gates or entrances. At the center of each temple is its highest and holiest place—a tower symbolizing both the sacred mountain of myth and the earthly power of the Khmers, who believed that by building their temples and palaces in the form of the mandala they were creating a link between their empire and the realm of divine power.

Angkor was the heart of the Khmer empire. The heart of Angkor was the six-square-mile walled imperial palace-city called Angkor Thom. And at the heart of Angkor Thom, Jayavarman VII built the temple known as the Bayon.

The Bayon is a nest of passageways and courtyards, a dense mass of stonework tapering upward to a rounded pinnacle. In 1928, one French conservator likened it to "a mountain peak that has been shaped and carved by human hands." Some of the Bayon's architectural oddities—such as hallways that lead nowhere and walls covered with sculptures where no one could possibly have seen them—suggest that plans may have been changed several times during the temple's construction.

The most remarkable feature of the Bayon is the faces. The temple complex contains many tall stone towers, from the tops of which immense carved faces, their lips curved in faint smiles, gaze serenely out on all four sides. There are 216 of these faces. Pierre Loti found them disconcerting:

> I raise my eyes to look at the towers which overhang me, drowned in verdure, and I shudder suddenly with an indefinable fear as I perceive, falling upon me from above, a huge, fixed smile; and then three, and then five, and then ten. They appear everywhere, and I realize that I have been overlooked from all sides by the faces of the quadruple-visaged towers.

By the time of King Jayavarman VII, on whose orders the Bayon was built, Buddhism had become the chief religion of the Khmers.

The mandala, seen here in a 17th-century Tibetan painting, is a sacred image to both Hindus and Buddhists, reflecting a holy landscape that is both geographical and spiritual.

The faces on the Bayon are believed to represent Buddha—and also the king, who identified himself with Buddha. A large statue of Buddha was excavated from the center of the Bayon; it may have covered Jayavarman's tomb. Less striking than the faces, but far more informative, are the many panels of carvings that adorn the walls of the Bayon. Many of these carvings illustrate scenes from religious mythology, such as battles between gods and demons. But others deal with the history of the Khmers, and some illustrate the everyday lives of ordinary folk, such as fishermen and stonemasons.

South of Angkor Thom is Angkor Wat, also surrounded by a moat. The temple covers about a square mile and has been called the world's largest stone monument and the world's largest religious shrine. Khmer records tell us that it took 37 years to build; the millions of sandstone blocks used in its construction were carried on rafts from a quarry 25 miles away.

Like Angkor Thom, Angkor Wat is laid out in the form of a mandala-like walled square. There is a tower at each corner and a taller (200-foot) tower in the center; these five towers represent the five peaks of Mount Meru. Sculptures on this temple depict Vishnu churning the milky ocean and other scenes from the *Mahabharata* and the *Ramayana,* the epic poems of Hinduism. Angkor Wat was originally dedicated to Vishnu. When it was later turned into a Buddhist temple, the central image of Vishnu was replaced with five Buddhas.

Other temples are scattered between and around Angkor Thom and Angkor Wat. Among these are Ta Prohm, which was dedicated to the mother of King Jayavarman VII. At one time, according to an inscription, this temple housed more than 5,000 priests, dancers, and other officials, all devoted to honoring

Many buildings at Angkor, including the temple of Ta Prohm, echo the mandala's center: a square sanctuary that can be entered through four gates.

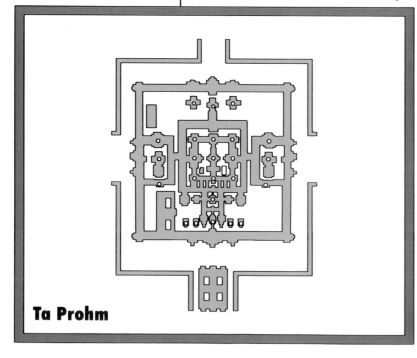

Ta Prohm

the memory of the king's mother. It was a wealthy temple. Among its goods were thousands of diamonds, pearls, and other gems, much gold and silver, and more than 2,000 elegant costumes for the statues. All of those sumptuous goods vanished long ago, of course. Ta Prohm was left untouched by the French conservators. Fig and kapok trees had acquired such a hold on its stonework that the conservators would

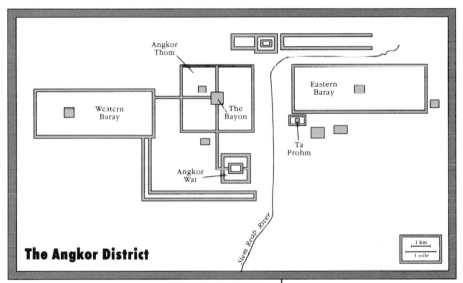

The Angkor District

have had to take the temple completely apart to remove them. So they left Ta Prohm to the roots, vines, and fire ants as an example of the state the ruins were in when conservation began.

The largest features of the Angkor district are two rectangular, artificial lakes called *barays*, located on either side of Angkor Thom. The Western Baray is more than half a mile wide and almost five miles long; the Eastern is somewhat smaller. Archaeologists used to think that the barays were originally quarries from which workers took foundation stones for the monuments of Angkor and for roadways throughout the Khmer lands. Today, however, the barays have been identified as reservoirs that may also have represented the mythical lakes said to surround Mount Meru.

Water was a key feature of life in Angkor and played an important part in the city's design. Temples were surrounded by moats and pools—not for protection, but so that they would be reflected in the water, doubling their impressiveness. These bodies of water were filled by a sophisticated irrigation system that drew water from nearby rivers into the barays and then funneled it throughout the district. The irrigation channels later became clogged, and some of the pools and reservoirs are now dry, but in the days of Angkor's glory its water-management system supported a population that may have been as high as a million. Ingenious use

The whole Angkor site resembles the symmetrical interior of a huge mandala, centered on the sacred squares of Angkor Thom and Angkor Wat.

of water resources allowed the Khmers to produce two or three rice harvests a year.

The modern era has been as hard on Angkor as the preceding centuries of neglect. The French conservators continued their work at Angkor after Cambodia became an independent nation in 1953. Angkor became a tourist attraction; luxury hotels were built nearby. But in 1970 Cambodia was engulfed in civil war. Tourism came to a halt, and the foreign conservators had to leave the country. Vietnamese forces invaded Cambodia in 1979 and remained in control of the country for a decade.

During the 1970s and 1980s, the Angkor district was the scene of much fighting between various factions. Rumors reached the outside world that monuments were being destroyed by gunfire, grenades, and vandals. Refugees streaming across the border into Thailand told of wholesale looting of the undefended ruins: Heads were removed from statues and sections of carvings were chiseled out of walls. Smugglers sold these items on the black market, and they ended up in the private collections of unscrupulous buyers around the world.

In 1986, the Vietnamese allowed a team of conservators from India to return to Angkor. The Indian team began cleaning the ruins with chemicals to remove lichens and moss and then sealing them with vinyl compounds in an attempt to keep new growth from forming. These efforts touched off an international controversy among experts in conservation, some of whom felt that the Indians' methods did more harm than good.

In 1989, Vietnam withdrew from Cambodia, and the United Nations started working with the various competing factions within Cambodia to form a coalition government. By the early 1990s, a degree of order had been restored to the country. Archaeologists, conservators, and tourists from many countries began returning to Angkor. They discovered that although war and vandalism had brought about some destruction at Angkor—sculptures shattered by bullets, for example, or statues smeared with paint—far greater damage had been done by the looting that continued unabated after the fighting stopped.

After visiting Angkor in 1993, anthropologist Russell Ciochon lamented that "thieves are looting Angkor so relentlessly that in time there may be little left to conserve." At that time the United Nations estimated that the site's artwork was being stolen at the rate of a piece a day. "The art thieves who come to Angkor now take photographs to show their customers," reported American archaeologist Richard Engelhardt. "They return to Thailand, where their clients make selections. I've been at a temple site where I've overheard Thai dealers discussing which pieces they're supposed to get for their clients." One enterprising group of thieves blasted into the archaeologists' storeroom with hand grenades and a rocket launcher and stole 22 stone artworks.

In 1993, representatives from 30 nations met in Tokyo to discuss ways to help Cambodia preserve its ancient Khmer heritage. Yet despite the fact that Angkor is once again becoming a tourist destination, the looting continues. Conservators are racing against time—and greed. Henri Mouhot's words, written in 1860, well describe Angkor's perilous condition today: "Unluckily the scourge of war, aided by time, the great destroyer, who respects nothing . . . has fallen heavily on the greater part of the monuments; and the work of destruction and decay continues among those which still remain standing, imposing and majestic, amidst the masses of ruins all around."

Two hundred sixteen faces of the Buddha gaze from the many towers and spires of the Bayon, a shrine in the center of Angkor Thom. Many of the faces are taller than a tall person.

CHAPTER 7

Troy
Myths and Treasures

*B*y the late 19th century, archaeology was emerging as a science in its own right. In Europe, Asia, Africa, and the Americas, antiquarians examined old ruins while eager searchers unearthed still more buried cities, homes, and tombs. But although archaeologists had uncovered many things of enormous artistic and historical value, none of them had yet found the sort of thing that most people call *treasure.* The discovery of Tutankhamen's gold-filled tomb in Egypt was still some years in the future; no archaeologist had ever discovered a really significant amount of gold. But in May of 1873, archaeology suddenly acquired the gleaming allure of treasure-hunting. Heinrich Schliemann found a priceless golden treasure buried in the ruins of the ancient city of Troy.

The story of Schliemann and Troy became one of the great legends of archaeology. Its ingredients are stirring: A passionate, self-educated amateur archaeologist who rose from poverty by his own efforts and had faith in his own ideas, even though the

An aerial view of Hissarlik, the hill in Turkey where Heinrich Schliemann discovered the fabled lost city of Troy. Archaeologists are still making important scientific discoveries at the site.

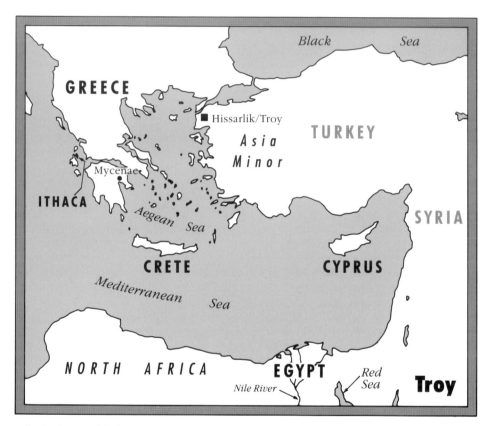

scholarly establishment told him he was wrong; clues hidden in an ancient epic poem written by a blind bard; a buried treasure and a desperate attempt to save it for science. Yet this popular legend does not tell the whole truth. Where both Troy and Schliemann are concerned, nothing is quite what it appears to be.

Few stories have survived as long as the tale of the Trojan War. In the 8th century B.C., the Greek poet Homer wrote two epic poems, the *Iliad* and the *Odyssey*, about events that had supposedly happened 500 years earlier, during the 13th century B.C. The *Iliad* tells how Paris, a prince of Troy, kidnapped Helen, the most beautiful woman in the world and the wife of a Greek lord named Menelaeus, and carried her across the Aegean Sea to Troy. King Agamemnon, Menelaeus's brother, assembled a vengeful force of Greeks, including the mighty warrior Achilles, and took them to Troy. The Greeks laid siege to the walled city, but King Priam of Troy did such a good job of defending his people that the siege dragged on for 10 years. The *Iliad* ends with a ferocious fight outside the city walls between Achilles and Hector, the Trojans' chief warrior. The story is picked up in the *Odyssey*, which tells how a small party of Greeks finally captured Troy by concealing themselves inside a large wooden horse. The unsuspecting Trojans wheeled the horse into their city, the Greek warriors poured out, and Troy was taken.

During the classical age of Greek civilization (700–200 B.C.), the story of the Trojan War was regarded as the early history of the Greek people. Achilles and Agamemnon were cultural heroes, and Troy was honored as the site of the Greek victory. Alexander the Great, on his way to fight the Persians in 334 B.C., was said to have stopped at Troy to make a sacrifice to the gods who had helped the Greeks overcome the Trojans. Like others of his era, Alexander accepted Homer's story as true in every detail. As for Homer, he was said to have been a blind poet, the inspired chronicler of the ancient Greeks. Later, when the Romans rose to dominate the Mediterranean world, they remained interested in the story of Troy, which they called Ilium. They built a city called Ilium Novum (New Troy) on what they believed to be the site of ancient Troy in northwestern Asia Minor, now Turkey. But by the 6th century A.D., the Romans had left Asia Minor, the city had fallen into disuse, and no one was sure exactly where Troy had been located.

By the 19th century, Troy and the Trojan War were no longer regarded as history; they had moved into the dim realm of myth or legend. The *Iliad* and the *Odyssey* were regarded as the first classics of Western literature, but no one seriously believed that they

A Greek wall carving shows Odysseus, one of Homer's heroes, returning home after the Trojan War and years of wandering. The early Greeks regarded Homer's epic poems as history. So did Heinrich Schliemann.

were literally true. Scholars had even begun to question Homer's existence. They suggested that the poems had been written not by a single poet, but by a number of individuals, perhaps over a long period of time, who simply polished and recorded traditional tales that had been passed down in spoken form from generation to generation. Historians were unable to trace Greek civilization further back than about the 8th century B.C. Before that, it seemed, the lands around the Aegean Sea had been inhabited only by poor, illiterate farmers—and there was no place in this dark prehistory for the magnificent cities and powerful kings that Homer had described. Such was the prevailing view in 1822, when Heinrich Schliemann was born in Germany.

In later years, Schliemann painted a touchingly sad picture of his childhood, and there is no doubt that his early life was not a happy one. His father was a pastor who was eventually dismissed by his church for drunkenness, adultery, and embezzlement. Even so, the elder Schliemann was a well-educated man who was interested in literature and history. He gave seven-year-old Heinrich a book that told the story of the Trojan War, with a picture of the great gate of Troy in flames. According to Schliemann's autobiography, this book had a profound effect on his young mind. Convinced that Troy must have been real, he vowed that when he grew up he would find it. The image of an impressionable child dedicating himself to discovering a legendary city is an appealing one, but recently a few scholars have taken a hard look at some of Schliemann's stories. Schliemann is now known to have played fast and loose with the truth on many occasions, and it is possible that he simply made up the story of his childhood obsession to make it seem that he had always been destined to find Troy.

The Schliemann family was so poor that Heinrich had to leave school at the age of 14 to work as a servant. When he was 19, he signed on as a cabin boy on a ship bound for South America, but the ship sank in a storm in the North Sea. Schliemann survived by clinging to a floating barrel until he was rescued. He then found a job as a clerk for a merchant firm in Amsterdam—a job that marked an upturn in his fortunes. With a good head for figures and the ability to teach himself languages quickly, Schliemann rose to the rank of manager in the company. He was sent to Russia, where he began amassing a fortune by trading in raw materials on his own account. In 1850 he went to California, which was then in the midst of a gold rush, and made nearly half a million dollars buying and selling gold dust. Upon his return to Moscow, he married a Russian woman, but the marriage was not a happy one, and when he left Russia in the 1860s his wife remained behind.

Schliemann kept making money. He invested in real estate, and he also reaped huge profits trading in military supplies during the Crimean War in Russia and the Civil War in the United States. In 1868, he visited Greece and Asia Minor. His first visit to the land of Homer was so inspiring that he retired from business to devote himself to the search for Troy. "I loved money indeed," he wrote, "but solely as the means of realizing this great idea of my life."

His guide would be Homer, for he had decided to treat the *Iliad* and the *Odyssey* as history, not poetry. Schliemann had fallen so deeply under Homer's spell that when he visited Ithaca, the Greek island where the hero of the *Odyssey* and his wife, Penelope, were said to have lived, he felt transported back in time: "Every hill, every stone, every stream, every olive grove reminded me of Homer, and so I found myself with a single leap hurled across a hundred generations into the glittering age of Greek knighthood." He hired four workmen to dig where tradition said Odysseus's palace had once stood. When the workmen found two jars filled with ashes, Schliemann reveled in the thought that the ashes were the remains of Odysseus and Penelope. Soon Schliemann would be just as quick to see "proofs" of Homer's accuracy on the other side of the Aegean Sea, in Turkey.

Two sites in northwestern Turkey were already vaguely associated with the legend of Troy. They were the village of Bunarbashi and a hill called Hissarlik. Schliemann marched around each with his copy of Homer's work in his hand and decided that Hissarlik more closely fit the references to Troy's location that he had found in the *Iliad*. A few people had already speculated that Hissarlik was the site of lost Troy, but Schliemann was convinced of it.

Before he could begin excavating at Hissarlik, Schliemann needed to obtain a firman, or permit, from the Turkish government. Realizing that at that time

After earning a fortune as a merchant, Heinrich Schliemann devoted his life to the search for Troy. Scholars are still debating Schliemann's honesty as well as his contributions to archaeology.

Turkey would grant a firman to an American more readily than to a German or a Russian, Schliemann spent 1869 in Indianapolis, Indiana, so that he could become a U.S. citizen. Schliemann's sojourn in the United States also allowed him to obtain a quick divorce from his Russian wife. He wanted to marry again, and by this time he was so devoted to Greek culture and history that only a Greek woman would suit him. He began asking friends to find suitable candidates. "She must be enthusiastic about Homer," he cautioned the matchmakers. The 47-year-old Schliemann chose one of the candidates, a 17-year-old girl named Sophia Engastromenos, and promptly married her. To the surprise of many of their acquaintances, the marriage turned out to be a happy, loving partnership.

In 1870, Schliemann returned to Hissarlik. He had not yet received his firman, but he began digging into the hill anyway. In the two weeks before the Turkish authorities called a halt to his illegal excavation, Schliemann uncovered parts of a stone wall, "six feet thick and of the most wonderful construction," he wrote excitedly. These, he was sure, were the walls of Troy that Homer had described.

Finally, the firman was granted, and Schliemann began work in earnest in 1871. He was furiously eager to discover Troy, and his methods were bold and impetuous. Rather than peeling away the 50-foot-tall mound of Hissarlik layer by layer, in the careful fashion that was beginning to be standard practice for serious archaeologists, Schliemann hired 120 workmen and ordered them to dig a wide, deep trench 130 feet long from one side of the mound to the other, like someone cutting a big slice through the middle of a cake to see what is hidden inside. Some said that he was proceeding as though he were digging the Suez Canal, not excavating an archaeological site.

The stone walls that Schliemann had found earlier were just the first layer of the cake. To Schliemann's surprise, he found not just Troy but a whole series of buried cities—layers of ruins stacked one on top of the other to a depth of about 45 feet. Each level clearly represented a city that had been built on the ruins of the city before it; the levels were separated by layers of earth. Several layers of ash indicated that some of the cities had been destroyed by fire. Schliemann had little interest in the upper levels, for he believed that the true

Troy, Homer's Troy, lay at or near the bottom. So, to the lasting regret of later archaeologists, he had his workmen ruthlessly cart away thousands of cubic yards of earth and rubble from the upper levels of the mound, destroying much valuable archaeological evidence in his haste to reach the bottom. "As it was my object to excavate Troy, which I expected to find in one of the lower cities, I was forced to demolish many interesting ruins in the upper strata," Schliemann said. His methods caused some scholars of his day to brand him "the second destroyer of Troy."

Schliemann's faith in the accuracy of Homer soared in 1873, when his diggers uncovered stone pavements and large earthenware jars near the bottom of the mound. In May they came upon the ruins of a large building, and Schliemann was convinced that he had found "the ruins of the palace of the last king of Troy, who is called Priam by Homer and all classical tradition." The climax of this season of great discoveries came at the end of May, when Heinrich Schliemann unearthed one of the most extraordinary finds ever made by an archaeologist: the golden treasure of King Priam.

According to Schliemann's account, he was digging in the foundations of "Priam's palace" when he saw the glint of gold in the dirt. To keep the workmen from seeing it, he hastily dismissed them. He did not want them to report the

Workmen at a tower on Troy VI, which dates from the period when the Trojan War is said to have taken place. If Homer's Troy did exist, these are its relics.

"Priam's treasure" was Schliemann's most impressive find and the most valuable treasure that had yet been discovered by any archaeologist.

gold to the authorities; his firman required him to turn over half of everything he found to the Turkish government, but Schliemann was determined to give all the important finds to Greece, which he had made his home. Once the workers were gone, Schliemann labored to uncover the gold, regardless of the danger from stone blocks balanced precariously overhead. He found a mass of golden objects packed close together, as though they had been inside a wooden box that had since rotted away. Sophia Schliemann smuggled the treasure away from the site in her red shawl. Later, in the cabin that they occupied at the top of the trench, they examined their haul and found that it consisted of a number of gold and silver drinking vessels, some silver ingots, and some tools. But the crowning glory was the gold jewelry: 3 headdresses, 60 earrings, half a dozen bracelets, and nearly 9,000 gold beads (which Schliemann later made into an impressive necklace). It was the most valuable archaeological discovery that anyone had made up to that time. The Schliemanns succeeded in smuggling the treasure out of Turkey to Greece, where Sophia's relatives hid it in their gardens and sheds until Schliemann was ready to reveal it to the world in 1874.

His revelation caused an uproar. The Turkish government was outraged and demanded the return of the treasure; archaeologists and scholars all over the world clamored for a look at the marvelous find; and to ordinary folk Schliemann the treasure hunter became an overnight hero. Priam's treasure turned into something of an embarrassment for Schliemann, however. He did not apologize for having tricked Turkey out of its share. At the time, it was standard practice for European archaeologists to plunder sites in Egypt and the Near

East, and many archaeologists prided themselves on their resourcefulness in doing so. But Schliemann was chagrined when the Greek government, under pressure from the Turks, refused to accept the treasure. Finally he sent it to Germany, and it was displayed in a state museum in Berlin. The Turkish government settled for fining him, and Schliemann, perhaps realizing that he had gotten off lightly, paid five times the amount demanded.

The fate of Priam's treasure became one of the greatest mysteries of modern archaeology. During World War II, Germany's art treasures, including the Trojan gold, were packed up and stored in bunkers for safekeeping. In the confusion of the war's end, when the victorious Russian and American armies occupied Germany, many of these treasures disappeared. Paintings, old books, jewelry, antiques, and other valuables were carried off, either looted by individual soldiers or seized as spoils of war by the victors. (Ironically, many of these treasures had been acquired by the Germans in exactly the same way.) The Trojan gold vanished from sight at this time. Historians mourned its loss, fearing that it had been melted down into gold ingots. All that remained were descriptions and photographs—including one haunting photograph of Sophia Schliemann wearing the headdress, earrings, and beads of a long-ago Trojan princess.

Not only had the treasure itself disappeared, but modern researchers began poking holes into Schliemann's account of how he had found it. The first claim to be challenged was the romantic image of Sophia smuggling the treasure away in her shawl; close examination of Schliemann's papers showed that Sophia had not even been at Hissarlik when the treasure was uncovered. Furthermore, Schliemann's various catalogues and descriptions of the treasure contradicted one another, leading some scholars to believe that the treasure was not a single find, as Schliemann had claimed. They suggest that he accumulated a number of smaller finds from various levels and locations at the site and later presented them as "Priam's treasure" in order to create a more dramatic impression.

The details of how and when Schliemann found the treasure will probably never be known, but the mystery of the treasure's fate has been solved. Rumors

Sophia Schliemann, adorned in the gold jewelry of ancient Troy. Heinrich Schliemann created the necklace from thousands of loose beads.

that the Trojan gold had been seen in Russia were confirmed in 1993, when the Russian government announced that Schliemann's treasure had been brought to Moscow after the war. As Turkey, Greece, Germany, and Russia launched a bitter squabble over the ownership of the treasure, the items discovered by Schliemann were prepared for an exhibition in Moscow in 1996—their first public display in more than half a century. Negotiations over the ownership of the Trojan gold may drag on for years, but archaeologists everywhere hope that these priceless and unique artifacts will soon be available for study.

Dramatic though it was, the discovery of the Trojan gold was just one incident in Schliemann's archaeological career. He continued to oversee the excavations at Hissarlik until his death in 1890, but in the mid-1870s he also excavated a Greek site called Mycenae, said by legend to have been the home of King Agamemnon, who conquered Troy. There Schliemann found a second and even more valuable treasure trove: a royal grave containing the gold-bedecked remains of a number of men, women, and children. One of the male skeletons wore a golden mask. "I have gazed upon the face of Agamemnon," Schliemann wrote with a mixture of pride and awe.

We now know that Schliemann was wrong about Agamemnon. The graves he found at Mycenae date from about 1600 B.C. Agamemnon, if he really existed, would have lived much later, at the supposed time of the Trojan War, around 1250 B.C. What Schliemann had uncovered at Mycenae was the first real evidence of a culture that flourished centuries before the rise of classical Greek civilization. The Mycenaean culture, as scholars call it in honor of Schliemann's site, dominated the Aegean Sea from about 1600 until about 1050 B.C. At the height of their power in the 14th and 13th centuries B.C., the Mycenaeans had settlements or trading stations throughout Greece, Crete, the Aegean islands, the coast of Turkey, and southern Italy. In about the 11th century B.C., the Mycenaean empire crumbled, and its people blended with tribes from the north to form the Greek civilization that blossomed in the 8th century. The language, literature, and religion of classical Greece preserved many elements of Mycenaean culture—including, most likely, legends of wars and kings that gave rise to the story of the Trojan War.

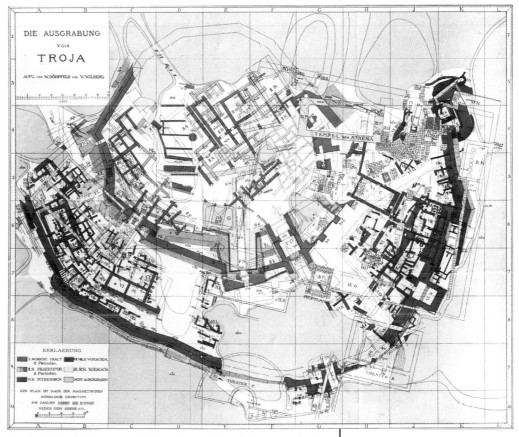

Schliemann was wrong about Troy, too. "Priam's treasure" came from a level of the excavation that modern archaeologists have dated to 2500–2200 B.C.—a thousand years before the era in which the Trojan War was supposed to have occurred, and thus long before King Priam's time. Hurrying toward the lowest levels of the site, where he believed Troy would be located, Schliemann had unwittingly dug right past the true level of Homer's Troy.

Much of the credit for sorting out the chronology of the various levels at Hissarlik goes to Wilhelm Dorpfeld, who Schliemann hired in 1882 to supervise the excavation. Dorpfeld established that the ruins consisted of nine distinct levels of settlement. He numbered them upward from Troy I, the deepest and oldest, through Troy IX, the uppermost and most recent. Schliemann believed that Troy II, where he had found the treasure, was the Homeric Troy— the Troy of the 13th century B.C. about which Homer had written. Dorpfeld believed that the site was much older than Schliemann had suspected and that the Homeric Troy would be found on a much more recent level, Troy VI. Although Schliemann was dismayed by the possibility that the treasure he had found might not have belonged to King Priam, he eventually accepted the evidence that Dorpfeld patiently gathered. Before his death he acknowledged that the artifacts he had discovered were a thousand years older than King Priam could have been.

Dorpfeld continued his work at Hissarlik after Schliemann's death and managed to locate parts of Troy VI that had not been destroyed by Schliemann's

A map of the excavation at Hissarlik shows overlapping layers of the many cities that stood on the site of Troy. The temple of Athena, at top right, was Greek, part of one of the more recent levels.

Schliemann's second extraordinary discovery, at Mycenae in Greece, included this golden mask, which he called "the mask of Agamemnon." The mask, however, was made hundreds of years before King Agamemnon lived—if he lived at all.

diggers. He discovered a large stone wall and evidence that Troy VI had been burned. This, Dorpfeld announced, was the *real* Troy. Modern experts have confirmed Dorpfeld's chronology: Troy I dates back to about 3000 B.C.; Troy II (Schliemann's Troy) dates to 2500–2200 B.C.; Troy VI dates from the 13th century B.C. (the period described in the *Iliad*); Troy VIII was the Greek city visited by Alexander the Great in the 4th century B.C.; and the top level, Troy IX, was the Roman town of Ilium Novum.

The next archaeologist to work at Hissarlik was an American, Carl Blegen, who arrived at the site in 1932. His methods reflected the 20th century's new, scientific approach to archaeology: He proceeded slowly and carefully, measuring, noting, and photographing everything before moving it. Digging in areas of the mound that had been left undisturbed by Schliemann and Dorpfeld, Blegen learned much about Troys III, IV, and V, but, like Schliemann and Dorpfeld before him, he was most interested in identifying Homer's Troy. Blegen subdivided Dorpfeld's 9 levels into 46 strata. One of the strata in Troy VII, he decided, was the likeliest candidate for the Troy of legend.

Today Hissarlik is nothing like the earth-covered hill that Schliemann began probing in 1870. It resembles a quarry, gouged by scores of pits and ditches, lined with crumbling stone walls that mark a succession of bygone cities. It has become one of Turkey's leading cultural attractions, drawing 300,000 tourists a year. Visitors are greeted by a three-story wooden horse, a symbol of the enduring Homeric legend; shows are presented in the theater that was built by the Romans in the 1st century A.D. Yet important scientific discoveries are still being made. A new series of expeditions, begun in 1988 by a team of German and American archaeologists, have found traces of a 10-foot-wide ditch that may have served as a defensive border around the hilltop. The ditch was cut deep into bedrock and encloses a large area, suggesting that some of the early cities on the site may have been five times as large as archaeologists had previously thought. Other recent finds include a larger-than-life marble statue of the Roman emperor Hadrian from Troy IX, and traces of a very early settlement below Troy I. Investigators have dubbed this prehistoric site Troy O, but as yet almost nothing is known about it.

The new excavations mark a significant change in the history of archaeology at Troy. For the first time, those working at the site are not guided by Homer and the *Iliad*. Manfred Korfmann, the German archaeologist in charge of the excavations, believes that it does not matter whether or not the events described in the *Iliad* ever happened. He has said, "I believe the *Iliad* contains a historical kernel of truth: that wars were constantly fought over this geopolitically important location. . . . The question of whether there ever was a Paris, or a Helen, must take a backseat."

Troy was clearly a power in the ancient world. It was located on a headland that overlooked an important trade route between Europe and Asia, the channel between the Mediterranean Sea and the Black Sea. At such an important crossroads of trade and travel, Troy was probably involved in a number of wars and sieges, and it is possible that the memory of these conflicts was carried through the centuries and inspired the Homeric stories. Unlike Schliemann, today's archaeologists view Troy as a historic site with a long and complicated history, not as proof of a literary legend's truth. "We are not proceeding from the *Iliad*," Korfmann explains. "We proceed, rather, as prehistorians from this highly interesting crossroads of cultures." Nevertheless, Heinrich Schliemann would surely be glad to know that one legend about Troy remains alive: the legend of the boy who dreamed over pictures of Troy in his childhood books and then grew up to find the city of myth, buried beneath the dust and oblivion of centuries.

On August 8, 1993, while restoring a theater built by the Romans, archaeologists found this marble statue of Hadrian, a Roman emperor of the 2nd century A.D.

CHAPTER 8

Zimbabwe
Great Houses of Stone

On September 4, 1871, a travel-weary explorer spent the night at the home of an African herdsman in Mashonaland, the home of the Shona people on the high plateau of south-central Africa, in what is today the nation of Zimbabwe. The traveler was a 34-year-old German named Karl Mauch, and he was hot on the trail of a legendary lost city. He had been told that large stone ruins lay only several hours' march away.

He rose early the next day and made his way forward over steadily rising ground, proceeding somewhat furtively so as to avoid attracting the attention of the local chieftain. Ahead loomed a solitary green hill with outcroppings of bare rock. Mauch drew closer and saw that the granite outcroppings were really the remains of huge buildings. "Presently I stood before it," he wrote in his journal, "and beheld a wall of a height of about 20 feet of granite bricks. Very close by there was a place where a kind of foot-path led over rubble into the

Part of a soapstone bowl (right) is one of the few artifacts found in these ruins at Great Zimbabwe. The discovery of the ruins touched off a long and bitter racial controversy.

Zambezi River

ZIMBABWE

Mashonaland

Great Zimbabwe ■

MOZAMBIQUE

MADAGASCAR

Kalahari Desert

Limpopo River

Indian Ocean

Durban

SOUTH AFRICA

Atlantic Ocean

Great Zimbabwe

interior. Following this path I stumbled over masses of rubble and parts of walls and dense thickets. I stopped in front of a towerlike structure." The tower, estimated Mauch, was about 30 feet tall. To his surprise, he found that the wall and the tower were made of slabs of rock precisely cut so that they would fit together with no trace of mortar, or cement, to hold them in place.

Mauch's journal entry that night was surprisingly calm, referring only to "the day which had been rich in surprises." Yet Mauch believed that he had made a remarkable discovery: He had found the biblical city of Ophir.

For centuries people had wondered about the location of the land of Ophir, the home of the Queen of Sheba. According to the First Book of Kings in the Bible, the gold mines of Ophir were the source of King Solomon's fabulous wealth. Ophir came to be associated with southeastern Africa after about the 10th century A.D., when Arabs trading in ports along the coast of southeastern Africa began obtaining gold that had made its way along trade routes from the interior to the coast.

In the 16th century, Portuguese explorers and invaders led by Vasco da Gama entered the Indian Ocean, seizing the ports along the African coast and taking control of the lucrative gold trade. They heard rumors of great cities and gold mines in the interior, ruled by an emperor called the Monomatapa or Benomotapa (European versions of the African words *mwene mutapa,* meaning "owner of the mines"). Writing in 1552, Portuguese historian Joao dos Barros said that he had been told of the Monomotapa's fortresses and towers, which were "built of stones of marvelous size," with no mortar joining the stones together. Such places, he said, were called "Symbaoe." The Portuguese associated these Symbaoe with the legendary Ophir, but made no attempt to find them; they were content to hold the coast and dominate trade.

Over the years, as Europeans mapped, traded, and conquered along the coast of Africa, tales of lost civilizations drifted like smoke out of the southeastern part of the continent. But by the mid-19th century, explorers were only beginning to probe inward from the coast, and geographic knowledge about the African interior was sparse. To Europeans, Africa was "the Dark Continent"—both because it was largely unknown, a place of mystery, and because they regarded the African people as primitive and barbarous. European maps of Africa featured large blank areas in the interior—blank areas that tantalized the imaginations of more than one future explorer.

In 1847, such a map came into the hands of 10-year-old Karl Mauch, the son of a carpenter in Stuttgart, Germany. By the age of 15, Mauch had dedicated himself to a life of exploration in Africa, determined to win glory by filling in some of those blanks on the map. As preparation, he studied biology, geology, and languages. He also steeped himself in the literature of exploration that flowed from the printing presses of Europe. Such mid-19th-century explorers as Richard Francis Burton, Samuel Baker, John Hanning Speke, and David Livingstone of Britain and Heinrich Barth of Germany all published accounts of their African expeditions, and these were widely circulated. At the age of 27, Mauch deemed himself ready to begin exploring. But as he had no official backing for an expedition and could not afford to equip one himself, he had to work his way to Africa as a member of the crew of a German freighter. The ship deposited him at Durban, a port on the southeastern coast of South Africa, which was then a British colony.

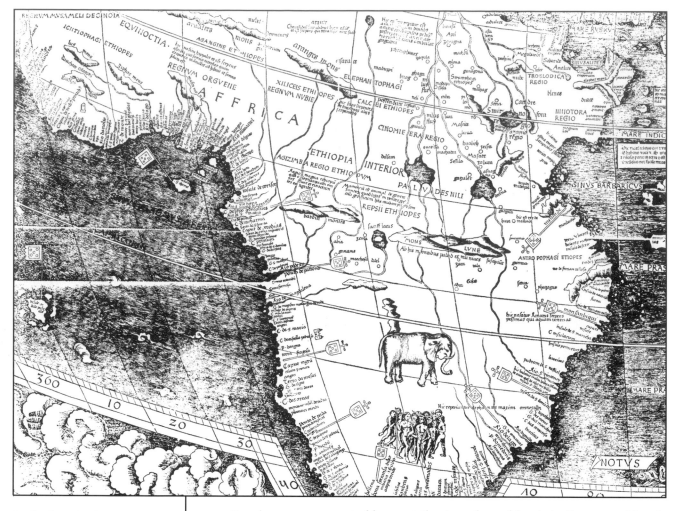

By the time Martin Waldseemüller made this map of Africa in 1507, European explorers had landed at scores of places around the continent's southern coast. The interior of southern Africa, however, remained blank on European maps for centuries.

For six years, supported by contributions from friends in Germany, Mauch crisscrossed southern Africa on foot. Unlike wealthier explorers, he did not hire a crew of African porters to carry his belongings. Clad in a leather suit he made from antelope hide, he carried all 60 pounds of his gear himself: a compass and sextant, a hunting knife, a blanket, a tin bowl, books, painting and writing equipment, a shotgun, and two revolvers. Laden with bags and parcels, with an enormous umbrella overhead serving as a sunshade, the burly, bearded Mauch was an impressive and strange sight as he strode across the savannah. South of the Limpopo River, Mauch saw geological formations that suggested that rich gold and diamond deposits might be found in the area. As required by British colonial law, he reported his find to local officials. Mauch's hunch was correct—both gold and diamonds are still being mined in that area.

Mauch soon met a German missionary named Adam Merensky, who had heard stories about giant stone ruins, the ancient capital of the Monomotapa, somewhere north of the Limpopo in Mashonaland. Merensky believed these ruins were those of the biblical Ophir, although he had never seen them. He shared his ideas about the ruins with Mauch, who was fired with enthusiasm for the quest. Surely the world would sing the praises of one who discovered the mysterious, ancient city described in the Bible.

There was another reason, too, for Mauch's enthusiasm: The Bible describes the Queen of Sheba and the land of Ophir as fabulously wealthy. When the Queen of Sheba came to Jerusalem to visit King Solomon, she was said to have brought with her "immense riches . . . great quantities of gold, and precious stones." Mauch probably had visions of finding a fortune in ancient gold and gems.

Mauch's expedition into Mashonaland was unusually well equipped; for once, the explorer had enough money on hand to hire porters. In May of 1871 he set off northward from Durban with about 40 men. Near the end of July, after crossing the Limpopo River, he made a journal entry that rings with German patriotism and archaeological ambition:

> In the sight of the reunited Fatherland, standing in forefront of all nations, and with the image of the Kaiser, crowned with victory, may now the most valuable and important, the hitherto most mysterious part of Africa be tackled, the old Monomotapa or Ophir!

A month later, Mauch found himself in dire straits. His porters had left him, carrying off some of his supplies as payment. To make matters worse, he feared that the local Shona people were hostile. He wrote somberly, "I had everything to fear here, not only the loss of my goods, but the loss of my life, either through poisoned food or by arrow." Mauch was rescued by Adam Render, a German hunter who had dropped out of white society and lived nearby with his two Shona wives. Mauch spent several days at Render's home, listening to Render's African friends talk about the ruins that lay only a dozen or so miles away on a hill called Zimbabwe or Zimbaoe. Mauch was certain that these ruins would prove to be the site that the Portuguese had called Symbaoe, the Monomotapa's fortress.

Karl Mauch dreamed of winning glory as an explorer but was doomed to disappointment and an early death.

Mauch filled his journal with descriptions and drawings of the artifacts, including a cracked stone bowl and a gong made of iron, that he found in the ruins of Great Zimbabwe.

It is not clear who accompanied Mauch on his final trek to the ruins; Render probably went with him, and at least one Shona guide as well. But it was Mauch who spent several days scrambling over the ruins, digging and sketching. Zimbabwe, he discovered, was huge. The tower he had first found at the site was only one of many ruined structures. Hillsides all around were dotted with roofless enclosures of stone, old walls, and towers. Despite the opposition of the local chieftain, who was suspicious of the white stranger's motives, Mauch made several visits to the site over the next few months.

Mauch was absolutely convinced that he had found Ophir. The most telling piece of proof, to his mind, was the reddish, fragrant piece of timber that formed part of the entrance to one of the ruins, a large round enclosure on a hilltop. Mauch cut a sliver from the beam, examined it, and decided that it was cedar. Recalling that the Bible mentions that Solomon used the cedar trees of Lebanon in building his palaces, Mauch leaped recklessly to the conclusion that this bit of

ZIMBABWE: GREAT HOUSES OF STONE   113

cedar must have come all the way from Lebanon. Therefore, he reasoned, it could only have been brought to Africa by the ancient seafaring people of the Lebanese coast, the Phoenicians. Furthermore, the Bible says that the Queen of Sheba visited Solomon's palace. Mauch decided that the round enclosure he had found on the hilltop had been built by none other than the Queen of Sheba herself, in imitation of Solomon's palace.

Mauch poked around in the ruins but found no trace of the Queen of Sheba's treasure. He did find a cracked bowl carved from soapstone and an iron gong, which he sketched in his journal with meticulous care. Mauch had no archaeological experience or training, however. The task of excavating the vast ruins was beyond him, and he feared for his safety if he lingered in the vicinity. In March of 1872, he packed up his gear and headed back across the Limpopo River to British-controlled territory.

Around that time the outside world was getting its first news of Mauch's find. Right after finding the ruins, Mauch had sent a messenger to the nearest European settlement bearing a letter to Germany. The letter, in which Mauch announced his find, was published in a German journal in March 1872, the same month that Mauch left the Zimbabwe region. It was the first official announcement in Europe that Zimbabwe had been found. By 1873, the news had been published in England, where a newspaper skeptically reported that "strange stories have been told of late about the Ophir of Solomon."

By then Mauch was back in Germany, where he published an account of his findings. His return was less triumphant than he had hoped. Not only was he *not* laden with treasure, but to his disappointment the discoverer of Ophir was not exactly showered with glory. Some people questioned whether Mauch had really found anything significant, while others regarded him as little more than a vagrant who had been lucky enough to stumble upon an archaeological discovery. The importance of that discovery, however, would be for others to determine. Karl Mauch could not even get a job in a university or museum because he lacked an academic degree. He went to work in a cement factory and died a few years later, in 1875, after falling from a window.

Great Zimbabwe's ruins are round, roofless stone enclosures, with thick, sloping walls and many round towers. Some modern researchers believe that the city's elite inhabitants lived in clay houses within these enclosures.

Mauch disappeared into obscurity, but over the next few decades the ruins at Zimbabwe became the center of an archaeological controversy. The first people to visit them were adventurers and treasure hunters, who went away disappointed because they found no hoards of gold or jewels. In 1899 the ruins, along with all of Mashonaland, passed into the hands of British financier Cecil Rhodes, who organized a company to settle the region. Within a few years the British had overcome the Africans' opposition and established a colony called Rhodesia.

Even before Rhodes's claim to Mashonaland was complete, he had ordered an investigation of Mauch's ruins. In the early 1890s, Rhodes's company and the British Association for the Advancement of Science sponsored the first scientific

THE RIDDLE OF RHODESIA ?

ZIMBABWE

A poster produced by the Rhodesian government in 1939 promoted the myth of white superiority and denied Great Zimbabwe's African origins.

study of the ruins, which had come to be called Great Zimbabwe. They hired James Theodore Bent, an expert on ancient civilizations, to make the arduous trek to the ruins. Bent expected to find evidence of Zimbabwe's link with ancient, exotic cultures, such as those mentioned in the Bible. At first he was disappointed, for Zimbabwe seemed to him to be African in origin and not very old. "I have not much faith in the antiquity of these ruins; I think they are native," he wrote. But when he discovered four large birds of carved soapstone, perched on tall carved pillars, he began to sing a different tune. These artifacts seemed to him to echo various ancient Mediterranean civilizations—Assyria, Greece, Crete, Egypt, Phoenicia. In short, they were anything but African. In his 1892 book *The Ruined Cities of Mashonaland*, Bent described the ruins as utterly alien to the landscape around them: "As a feature in the country they are most remarkable—ancient, massive, mysterious, standing out in startling contrast to the primitive huts of the barbarians who dwell around them and the wilderness of nature." This is the image that haunted the imagination of British novelist H. Rider Haggard, whose 1895 adventure novel *King Solomon's Mines* was based on tales of Zimbabwe.

Bent's successor as the official archaeologist of Zimbabwe was Richard N. Hall, who worked at the site from 1902 to 1904. Hall's methods were destructive, rather like those of Heinrich Schliemann. He was eager to restore the ruins to what he believed was their "original" state, so he ruthlessly cleared 12 feet of dirt and rubble from the interior of the towers—thus destroying everything that other, more careful archaeologists might have learned about Great Zimbabwe's history from a scientific study of the artifacts buried in the rubble. In the end, Hall's conclusions tallied with Bent's: Zimbabwe had been built by northerners from Arabia or the Near East, people who were, as Hall put it, "the more civilized races of the ancient world."

Bent, Hall, Rhodes, and other Europeans of the time were more than ready to be persuaded that Zimbabwe was not of African origin. European territorial claims, missionary enterprises, and economic ventures in Africa were based upon the central belief that Africans were inferior beings whose own wishes could be disregarded and who needed the "guidance" of more civilized cultures. At the time, most Europeans believed that all Africans south of the Sahara Desert had always lived in mud huts—a sure sign of primitiveness. The notion that an African civilization might have been sufficiently well organized and creative to build the impressive stone structures at Great Zimbabwe threatened Europeans' comfortable sense of superiority. Thus this idea indirectly attacked the very presence of Europeans in Africa. For this reason, the British and their colonists in Rhodesia had a large stake in believing that Great Zimbabwe was not African.

Scholars, politicians, and cranks turned out a bewildering variety of ever more fanciful theories to account for the ruins. Great Zimbabwe had been built not by Phoenicians but by exiles from the court of the Egyptian pharaohs. Or Arabs from North Africa. Or by the Lost Tribes of Israel, mentioned in the Bible. Or by shipwrecked Vikings. In 1936, the curator of the ruins wrote that it was "almost impossible" to imagine that black Africans could have created Great Zimbabwe—although he suggested that Africans had been used as "beasts of burden" by the real builders. A poster produced in 1938 by the Rhodesian government bluntly expresses the point of view of the country's white rulers: A black man kneels before the ruins, which are white. He offers a large nugget of gold to a ghostly apparition who is supposed to represent the Queen of Sheba. She is, of course, white.

By this time, however, the notion that Great Zimbabwe was the relic of a "white" civilization was under serious attack. The truth about the ruins had been known for years. As early as 1905, a well-known archaeologist named David Randall-MacIver had examined the ruins carefully and echoed Bent's first verdict. Great Zimbabwe, he declared, was "unquestionably African in every detail." The British Association for the Advancement of Science, unwilling to accept this conclusion, sent another top archaeologist, Gertrude Caton-Thompson, to prove Randall-MacIver wrong. Caton-Thompson conducted an extremely thorough

study of the site in 1929 and announced that Randall-MacIver was right. The ruins were African.

Still the controversy raged on. Many whites, including some scientists, were simply unwilling to believe that black people could have built the ruins. As late as 1970, the government archaeologist of Rhodesia was forced to resign because he agreed with the archaeological evidence that Great Zimbabwe was African. Ten years later, however, when Rhodesia became an independent nation with full rights for its black majority population, the country's name was proudly changed to Zimbabwe, making it the only country in the world named for an archaeological site. The name is a version of the Shona words *dzimba woye,* meaning "honored houses."

Today, few archaeologists or scholars would question the overwhelming weight of evidence that Great Zimbabwe was built by the ancestors of the modern Shona people. In fact, modern researchers have discovered that Great Zimbabwe was the center of a powerful African state that once dominated the Zimbabwe Plateau, the fertile highland between the Limpopo River on the south

The geology of the Zimbabwe plateau helped the builders of Great Zimbabwe. The local granite split naturally into thin sheets, which stoneworkers cut into building blocks. The smooth blocks fit together so well that they could be stacked into high walls and towers.

and the Zambezi River on the north. To the west of the Zimbabwe Plateau is a vast rolling plain that gradually becomes drier and drier until it turns into the arid Kalahari Desert of southwestern Africa. To the east, a lowland plain forms the border between the Zimbabwe Plateau and the Indian Ocean.

The early Shona found the Zimbabwe Plateau a hospitable place to live. Temperatures were moderate, rainfall was abundant, and the sweeping grasslands provided plenty of grazing for livestock. The people of the plateau developed an economy based on cattle. Wealth was measured by the size of a herd, and cattle were a medium of exchange, used to purchase goods. However, although the people of the plateau measured their own wealth in cattle, they had other goods to trade with the outside world. Mines in the area yielded copper, iron, tin—and gold, which soon became the major export of the plateau. By the 9th century A.D., a pattern of trade had developed. Gold flowed eastward from Zimbabwe into the hands of African and Arab traders in the ports that dotted the African coast from present-day Kenya south through Mozambique. In return for the gold, these merchants sent goods from other parts of their vast trading empire westward into the African interior. At Great Zimbabwe, archaeologists have found coins from the East African port of Kilwa, ceramic ware from China, glass beads from India, and a pottery bowl from Iran.

The gold trade brought wealth into the cattle kingdoms of the Zimbabwe Plateau, and by the 11th century this new wealth had begun to reshape the Shona economy. An elite ruling class of kings and nobles emerged. At Shona settlements across the plateau, these aristocrats adopted the custom of building their residences on top of hills, leaving the lower classes to settle on the lower slopes and in the valleys. The wealthy noble families also began enclosing their districts within stone walls. These walls were not intended to protect the nobles from attack; rather, the walls were a sign of the nobility's separateness from ordinary folk.

Stone for the walls was easy to find, because the Zimbabwe Plateau has many outcroppings of granite. The Shona based their style of stonework on an unusual feature of the Zimbabwean granite: The contrast between cold nights and hot days causes the granite to crack and split naturally into thin sheets. Shona stoneworkers learned to speed up this cracking process by lighting fires

on the rocks and then drenching them with cold water. They also speeded up the splitting process by driving wedges into the cracks, producing slabs of rock that could be peeled away from the hillside in smooth, flat sheets. The Shona developed a type of architecture that was ideally suited to these building stones: thick walls built of layer upon layer of flat stones that were smooth enough to fit snugly together without mortar to hold them in place.

Great Zimbabwe was not the only Shona settlement on the plateau, or even the first. Modern archaeologists have found traces of as many as 150 circular stone enclosures, and they believe that perhaps 50 more have been destroyed since the beginning of the 20th century. Some of these sites are small and probably housed no more than 20 people. Others are much larger. The largest and most powerful was Great Zimbabwe.

Researchers have found signs that the site of Great Zimbabwe was temporarily occupied, probably by wandering herdspeople or hunters, as long ago as the 4th century A.D. The first permanent settlement on the site probably occurred in the 10th or 11th century. By about 1250, when Great Zimbabwe was regularly supplying gold to the trading ports on the coast of Mozambique, the city reached the peak of its size and importance. It dominated the Zimbabwe Plateau for the next 200 years. The great stone structures that still stand today were built during this period.

The ruins of Great Zimbabwe cover about 100 acres and are in three main parts. The Hill Ruin is a cluster of stone walls forming enclosures on top of a hill. Archaeologists today believe that these enclosures were the domain of the city's highest-ranking inhabitants—royalty and perhaps priests. Within the Hill Ruin

Built on the wealth of its gold mines, Great Zimbabwe was the center of a trading empire that reached from the interior of Africa to the Indian Ocean. Goods from Iran, Arabia, India, and China have been found in the city's ruins.

excavators have found a number of the carved soapstone birds. These are thought to have been symbols of links between the living Shona kings and the spirits of dead kings, emblems of both religious and political power.

Below the Hill Ruin is the Great Enclosure, an oval 300 feet across. The Great Enclosure contains several smaller stone enclosures and a 30-foot tower and is ringed by a dozen similar but much smaller oval enclosures. No one is sure exactly what purpose these enclosures served, but one modern researcher has suggested that it was a sort of school, a place in which young people were prepared for adulthood and marriage. The smaller enclosures outside the Great Enclosure may have been the homes of wealthy citizens or of priests and teachers connected with the "school."

The third part of the site consists of relics of the town that filled the spaces around and between the Hill Ruin and the Great Enclosure. Here the common people lived in circular houses made of *daga,* a type of cement formed by mixing gravel with a damp clay found in termite mounds. The houses may have been roofed with timber or tree branches. *Daga* was also used to build the houses inside the stone enclosures, where the elite lived.

Great Zimbabwe's stone ruins, built of local granite, are massive. The walls are hollow, constructed of an inner wall and an outer wall, both sloping inward from bottom to top for greater strength. The space between the inner and outer walls was filled with stones and rubble. The wall of the Great Enclosure is from 20 to 33 feet high and in places is 15 feet thick at the bottom. It is 800 feet in length and contains nearly a million granite blocks. Steps and doorways are set into the stonework with great precision, and in some places stones of varying colors or textures have been used to create zigzag patterns in the walls. These designs greatly resemble the patterns that many people in southern Africa paint on the walls of their homes today.

The Shona used no written language. Without documents or inscriptions, archaeologists may never know for certain how the various buildings were used or what everyday life was like for the people of this Zimbabwean state. Recent work at the site, however, has provided some clues. Early researchers believed that Great Zimbabwe had between 1,000 and 2,500 inhabitants, but evidence

encouraged to collect and study ancient coins. Young Evans went to college at Oxford University in England and Göttingen University in Germany. After college he traveled in Eastern Europe, wrote several books about that region, married, and settled into a 25-year career as the curator of the Ashmolean Museum at Oxford University. With energy and vision, Evans transformed the Ashmolean from a dusty, half-forgotten collection of artifacts into a dynamic leader among the world's museums. His job gave him a great deal of free time, however, during which he continued to travel and to carry out his own research.

In 1883, during a tour of Greece, Evans and his wife visited Schliemann at his home in Athens. Schliemann proudly displayed his Mycenaean finds, including a number of seals—small rings or pieces of carved stone bearing designs that were pressed into clay or wax. When Evans took a close look at the seals, a peculiarity of his own eyesight served him well. Evans was extremely nearsighted, which was a handicap when he tried to look at things far away, but his ability to make out the details of very close objects was phenomenal. Examining the Mycenaean seals, Evans saw what no one else had noticed: many of the symbols and pictures seemed alien to Mycenaean and Greek culture. Some of the carvings on the seals were images of marine life, such as a tiny octopus. These images were unlike anything Evans had seen in Greek or Mycenaean artifacts. Other symbols on the seals resembled Egyptian hieroglyphic writing and the mysterious symbols found on some Mycenaean jars.

Evans knew that scholars had already pointed out a few designs and other elements in Mycenaean relics that simply did not seem to fit in with the "Mycenaean style." Historians had suggested that these elements were traces of some other, unknown culture that had influenced or interacted with the Mycenaeans. Now Evans thought that Schliemann's seals might be a clue to this unknown culture. He went still further and speculated that the markings on the seals might represent the origin of written language in Europe.

In the years that followed, Evans collected a number of similar seals from sites around the eastern Mediterranean. Curio dealers from places as far apart as Athens, Greece, and Cairo, Egypt, told him that the seals came from Crete, a large island 65 miles south of Greece. Evans knew that fragments of pottery had

been found at a large mound called Kephala near the northern coast of Crete. Legends identified Kephala with Knossos, the palace of the Cretan king Minos. According to ancient Greek literature, King Minos sacrificed young Athenian men and women to the Minotaur, a fearful monster, half human and half bull, that lived in a huge labyrinth, or maze, at Knossos. In the legend of the Minotaur and the maze, the Athenian hero Theseus was saved by Ariadne, daughter of King Minos, who showed him how to escape from the labyrinth.

Evans was not the first antiquarian to speculate about the Cretan past, however. After his triumphs at Troy and Mycenae, Heinrich Schliemann had turned his attention to Crete. Schliemann took ancient legends seriously. He had already found one lost city—Troy—by following the clues in the ancient epic poem the *Iliad*. The *Iliad*'s sequel, the *Odyssey*, recounts the adventures of a band of Greek heroes after the fall of Troy. The *Odyssey* describes Crete: "Out in the dark

Sir Arthur Evans devoted three decades to excavating and restoring the palace at Knossos. His labors brought him a knighthood and aroused worldwide interest in the Minoans.

blue seas there lies a land called Crete, a rich and lovely land, washed by the waves on every side, densely peopled and boasting ninety cities. . . . One of the ninety towns is a great city called Knossos, and there . . . King Minos ruled and enjoyed the friendship of almighty Zeus." Schliemann believed that the legend of King Minos and Knossos, like the legend of Troy, had some basis in fact. He walked over Kephala, seeing pottery fragments and bits of shaped stone sticking up through the earth, and yearned to follow up his triumphs at Troy and Mycenae by excavating the palace of King Minos. In 1888, two years before his death, Schliemann wrote, "I would like to end my life's labours with one great work—the prehistoric palace of the kings of Knossos in Crete." But he was unable to purchase Kephala from its owners and gave up the plan.

Evans was luckier. On his first visit to Crete, in 1894, he was staggered by the number of ancient carved sealstones he saw in shops or worn around peasants' necks as charms. Convinced that Crete held buried archaeological secrets, he set about the tiresome task of haggling with the owners of Kephala. Fortunately for Evans, several of the owners were Turks, and in the late 1890s the Cretan people rose up against their Turkish rulers and drove them from the island. By 1900, Evans was in possession of Kephala. His wife had died a few years earlier. Forty-eight years old and childless, Evans was ready to devote himself to a new enthusiasm. He had no experience in excavation, but he had plenty of time, energy, and money. He hired a crew of local men and started digging.

Some hopeful archaeologists dig and dig, excavating for months or even years before their search is rewarded. Not Evans. On the first day, he and his excavators found building walls and artifacts. On the second, they found a wall with frescoes, or decorations painted on plaster, that were faded but still visible. By the fifth day, the site bristled with stonework—it seemed that every spade struck into the ground at random brought to light another ruin. Kephala was filled with ruins, so lightly buried that they were practically bursting out of the ground. The finds piled up: dozens of carved seals; vases; clay jars as tall as a man that had stored grain, wine, and oil; and hundreds of clay tablets inscribed with writing in two unknown languages, which Evans named Linear A and Linear B because they used symbols made of straight lines.

From the start, Evans knew that he had opened a new chapter in history. The ruins he was excavating were unlike anything seen before. Four days after the digging started, he wrote in his journal, "It's an extraordinary phenomenon, nothing Greek, nothing Roman. . . . Maybe its greatest period goes back to at least well before the pre-Mycenaean period." Another fresco was uncovered, and this one bore a life-size picture of a graceful, black-haired man wearing a belted loincloth. Evans had seen pictures just like it before, in Egypt, where wall paintings from the days of the pharaohs showed people dressed in similar clothing and bearing gifts. The Egyptians had called them *Keftiu,* or "people of the islands." Evans was sure that the Keftiu and the builders of Knossos were one and the same. Later evidence would show that he was correct and that the Cretans enjoyed a friendly trading relationship with the Egyptians.

In just one month of digging, Evans and his crew discovered that the ruins were not separate buildings. They were all part of a single huge structure that archaeologists later termed a palace-complex. Evans's first season of excavation uncovered more than two acres of this structure; ultimately it would be found to cover more than six acres and to have more than 1,400 rooms. A many-leveled nest of rooms, courtyards, passages, stairways, basements, and balconies, the palace-complex did indeed resemble a maze in which the unwary could easily become lost. This, decided Evans, must be

An octopus peers from the painted design on a clay storage jar that Evans found at Knossos. Minoan pottery, wall paintings, and seals are rich in images of under-sea life.

Evans (at the top, in white) with his crew at the palace's Grand Staircase, which he ordered rebuilt.

the origin of the labyrinth legend. Evans even believed that he had found a throne room: a magnificently painted chamber on the west side of the mound, with stone benches along the walls and a single stone seat, higher than all the rest. When Evans announced his discoveries to the world, he christened the inhabitants of the site Minoans, after King Minos.

Evans's announcement caused a sensation. The finds at Knossos, the London *Times* declared, "equal, if they do not surpass, in importance the discoveries of Schliemann." Realizing that Evans had found not just a ruin but a whole new civilization, archaeologists from many universities and museums hurried to Crete.

They set to work excavating every place that had a legend or folktale associated with it and every mound of earth. Soon the island was as overrun with archaeologists and their diggings as an untended garden is with moles and molehills.

The work at Knossos continued under Evans's direction. In 1901 he made more discoveries: a staircase on one side of the large central courtyard; more wall paintings with scenes of religious rites and daily life; and a game board made of ivory, silver, gold, and crystal. The board suggests that the ancient Minoans played games that relied on a combination of skill and chance. Evans later called the game board the single most magnificent artifact ever found at Knossos.

In 1906, Evans built a house near the site, where he could live in comfort and entertain distinguished visitors while continuing his work. His labors at Knossos lasted for 30 years and brought him worldwide renown; in 1911 he was knighted for his contribution to archaeology. He summed up his decades of study at Knossos in *The Palace of Minos*, published in four volumes from 1921 to 1935. Although some of Evans's conclusions are now known to have been wrong, and many important discoveries have been made in recent years, his work remains the foundation of Minoan studies.

Evans realized that people had lived at the site of Knossos long before the palace was built. He dated the earliest traces of residence to 8000 B.C., but more recent studies indicate that the oldest settlements at Knossos date from about 6000 B.C. A culture recognizable as Minoan emerged around 2500 B.C. At this time the Cretans probably lived in small villages. Over time, their society grew more centralized. People began to congregate in larger, more structured communities. Knossos, set in the middle of a broad valley with plenty of water and good farmland, was the ideal setting for such a community. Elsewhere in Crete, other population centers formed.

By about 1900 B.C., Minoan society had entered a phase that archaeologists call the Old Palace period. During this period, they built large palaces at Knossos and also at Mallia and Phaistos, sites that were discovered after Evans began his excavations. The Old Palace era lasted until about 1700 B.C., when the palaces were destroyed by a severe earthquake; the Minoans rebuilt them. During the New Palace period, which lasted from 1700 until about 1470 B.C., the Minoan civilization reached its economic and artistic height. In the New Palace period, the Minoans built a fourth palace, at Zakros, on the southeastern coast of Crete. Archaeologists have discovered hundreds of Minoan sites on the island, ranging from the four large palace-complexes to small towns, villages, and country estates.

Knossos was the largest of the Minoan palaces, which were unlike anything archaeologists had ever seen. They were not simply royal residences or symbols of state power. Each was essentially a town under a single sprawling roof, with streets, storerooms for food and trade goods, workrooms for artisans, residences, ceremonial chambers, and shops, all radiating outward from a central court. The palaces grew over time as new passages, rooms, and staircases were added at the outer edges. These lavish dwellings were probably crowded, but they appear to have been surprisingly sanitary; the Minoans had some of the best plumbing in the ancient world. Knossos had bathing pools, pipes to bring in fresh water, and at least one toilet. Scholars coined the term palace-complex to describe Knossos and the other Minoan centers because the royal rooms themselves formed only a small part of the total structure. Very little is known about the Minoan government or any of the Minoan rulers; scholars do not even know whether Minos was a particular king or a name used by a whole dynasty of rulers, as Evans believed. But it seems clear that Minoan society was highly organized. Only a unified, cooperative culture could have built and maintained Knossos and the other palace-complexes.

Minoan influence extended far beyond the island of Crete. The Minoans were skilled navigators with an efficient fleet of ships. Vessels of the New Palace

period were up to 100 feet long and were staffed by crews of 50. They were easily capable of crossing the eastern Mediterranean. In all likelihood, the Minoans established colonies or trading posts on a number of the islands in the Aegean Sea between Greece and Turkey. Around 1500 B.C., the Minoans began to ornament their pottery and sealstones with images that celebrated their link with the sea: dolphins, octopuses, and shellfish in natural-looking settings of seaweed and rock.

The Minoan economy was based on trade. Minoan artifacts, such as sealstones, have been found all over the eastern Mediterranean. Metals, gemstones, pottery, ivory, and other goods from Greece, Turkey, the Aegean islands, Egypt, and Mesopotamia have been found at Minoan sites. Archaeologists working in Crete have also found multitudes of the enormous jars that were once used for storing olive oil and wine, two products that the Minoans exported. The Minoans also exported timber, wool cloth, pottery, jewelry, knives, and perfumes and medicines.

Much of what archaeologists and scholars have told us about the Minoans is careful guesswork. We know a great deal more about the ancient Egyptians who lived while Minoan civilization was flourishing than we do about the Minoans. This is because we can read the documents and inscriptions left behind by the Egyptians—but not those of the early Minoans. Arthur Evans spent decades trying to decipher the symbols of Linear A and Linear B. He failed. Lin-

Evans believed that this was the throne of King Minos. Scholars today believe that the "throne room" may really have been a shrine to several priestesses.

Little is known of the Minoan religion. The female figure holding serpents probably represents a goddess or priestess. In other portrayals she holds a double-bladed axe. Such axes may have been used in sacrifices of animals—or of people.

ear A was found only in Minoan sites in Crete, but Linear B was associated with Mycenaean sites and relics as well as Minoan ones. Evans and other scholars assumed that Linear A was the written Minoan language and Linear B the Mycenaean language, but both scripts baffled the most earnest efforts to decipher them. A clay disk found at Phaistos provided a third type of Minoan writing—symbols of animals, birds, people, and ships, probably stamped into the damp clay with seals.

In 1952, Michael Ventris, a British architect who had been interested in Minoan culture ever since hearing Evans lecture in his boyhood, brought the scholarly world to attention with the announcement that he had decoded Linear B. Scholars since Evans had believed that both Linear A and Linear B were wholly new languages. But Ventris had wondered whether the Mycenaean language might be an early form of Greek—and he found that it was. He was able to identify the symbols of Linear B with words in Greek, proving that the language expressed in Linear B, the script of the Mycenaeans, was an ancestor of the modern Greek language.

Linear A has yet to be deciphered, although linguists and cryptographers have tried every known decoding method, including elaborate computer programs. The Minoan language remains a mystery. If scholars ever succeed in cracking Linear A, many lingering questions about the Minoans may be answered.

The religion of the Minoans, like their government, is largely a matter of conjecture. Evans and later archaeologists have found many statues and frescoes of women believed to be either goddesses or priestesses. Archaeologists today believe that the supreme deity of the Minoans was a goddess and that women played important roles in Minoan religious rituals. In fact, the room that Evans thought was a throne room is now thought to be a shrine where women worshipped the goddess.

The priestesses or goddesses portrayed in Minoan art often hold snakes or double-bladed axes. These axes occur over and over again in Minoan artwork and may have been connected with animal sacrifices—one fresco shows a bull being sacrificed to the gods. Evans uncovered scores of images of bulls: drinking vessels in the shapes of bull heads, frescoes and statues of bulls, bulls' horns decorating everything from gateways to jars. Most startling were the paintings and statues that depicted young Minoan men and women engaged in what appears to be an extremely dangerous stunt: leaping between the horns of a charging bull and somersaulting over its back. Scholars are still not certain whether this bull-leaping, as it has been called, really took place as it is portrayed, or what its significance was. It is possible that dangerous ceremonies involving young athletes and bulls formed the basis of the legend of the Minotaur that devoured youths and maidens.

Evans's discovery of the Minoans captivated the public as well as the scholarly world. One of the most fascinating aspects of the Minoans was their artwork. Their lively, naturalistic images seemed somehow more human, or at least more modern, than the stiff, formal, often rather grim artworks of other ancient civilizations, such as the Assyrians and the Babylonians. The Minoans portrayed themselves as a smiling, gracious people who loved the natural world and enjoyed games. They even seemed fashionable. Men and women alike wore their long black ringlets pinned up in back. The men wore loincloths; the women wore red lipcoloring, long flounced skirts, and tight bodices that left their breasts bare. In all, the Minoans seemed a spirited, cultured, and peaceful people. During the first half of the 20th century, an image arose of Minoan Crete as an idyllic, golden-age place.

Recent discoveries have cast something of a shadow over this idealized image. For a long time, archaeologists believed that the Minoans were pacifists, with no army and no fortifications around their palaces, but now it is known that they possessed swords, spears, and daggers and that some of their settlements may have been fortified.

Minoan religion may also have had its dark side. One of the most controversial discoveries of modern archaeology took place in 1979. Greek archaeologists Efi and Jannis Sakellaris were excavating Minoan ruins in northern Crete. At a place called Anemospilia—"caves of the wind"—by the local Cretans, the

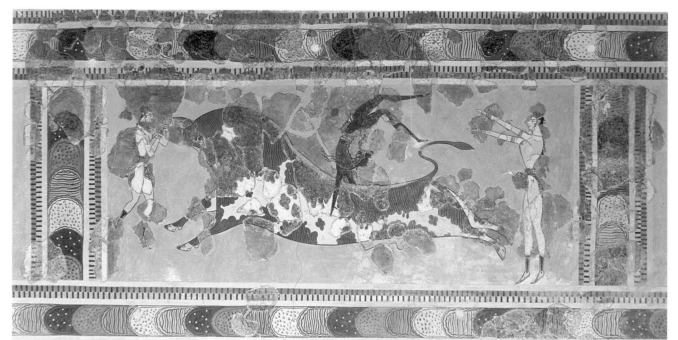

If the Minoan stunt called "bull-leaping" really took place, it may have been a religious ritual performed by both men and women. Scholars believe that Minoan artists drew men as dark figures and women as pale ones.

Sakellarises found a small structure that they thought had probably been a shrine. It appeared to have been destroyed in an earthquake in about 1550 B.C. Inside the shrine they found remnants of a life-sized statue, possibly of the supreme goddess, and a vase that might have held sacrificial blood. Vases like it appeared in frescoes, where they caught the blood of sacrificed bulls. The chamber also contained the first Minoan bodies that have ever been discovered outside tombs. Altogether, there were four skeletons. Three had been crushed by the earthquake that destroyed the shrine. The fourth, later determined to be that of an 18-year-old man, appeared to have been bound and ritually sacrificed. A ceremonial knife lay across his remains.

The Sakellarises suggested that the youth had been sacrificed, perhaps to ward off the earthquake. The idea that the Minoans—long thought of as more peaceful and gracious than many other inhabitants of the ancient world—had practiced human sacrifice stirred up a storm. The people of Greece and Crete were dismayed by what many felt was an insult to their ancestors. In a public meeting in Athens in 1980, archaeologists debated the Sakellarises' discovery. Most were inclined to think that the Sakellarises had misinterpreted their find.

Four years later, however, an even more sensational discovery seemed to indicate that the Sakellarises had been on the right track after all. While excavating a basement room in a Minoan building northwest of Knossos, British archaeologist Peter Warren found the bones of two children, aged 8 and 11. Knife marks on the bones were identical to those on the bones of sacrificial animals. The bones and other evidence suggested to Warren that the children had been ritually killed. The flesh had then been stripped from their bones. Warren believes that worshippers may have eaten the flesh of the two sacrifices. His theory remains highly controversial, but even skeptical archaeologists now agree that our earlier, sunny images of Minoan culture and worship need to be revised.

Minoan civilization reached a crisis in 1470 B.C., when all the palaces except Knossos, and all the outlying settlements and villas, were burned. Evans believed that the Minoans had been wiped out by an earthquake. In 1926, another earthquake struck Knossos, making a powerful impression on Evans, who wrote, "A dull sound rose from the ground like the muffled roar of an angry bull." It seemed logical to Evans that earthquakes, which regularly shake Crete and other Aegean islands, might have helped create the legend of the Minotaur in his underground labyrinth. Earthquakes could also have brought the Minoan civilization to its end.

More signs of natural disaster emerged in the mid-20th century, when archaeologists began excavating ruins on the Aegean island of Thera, formerly called Santorini. At a place called Akrotiri on the southern coast of Thera, they discovered a buried city filled with artifacts and frescoes very similar to the Minoan relics on Crete; Akrotiri, it seemed, had been either a Minoan outpost or a community closely linked by trade and cultural ties to the Minoans. Geological evidence showed that Akrotiri and possibly other communities were destroyed in a huge volcanic explosion around the year 1600 B.C. The eruption on Thera may have given rise to the ancient Greek tale of the island of Atlantis, an advanced society destroyed by a natural disaster. Some researchers also thought that it explained the destruction of the Minoans. The cataclysm on Thera, they speculated, might have blanketed Crete with volcanic ash or swamped its coastal settlements with huge tidal waves.

Modern scholars have rejected the idea that Minoan civilization was wiped out by a single natural disaster. Instead, they believe that the Minoans became involved in a power struggle with the emerging Mycenaean civilization of mainland Greece, and that the Mycenaeans took control of Crete, destroyed nearly all

In reconstructing Knossos, Evans drew upon what he thought he knew about the Minoans as well as upon the physical evidence. Some modern experts feel that this famed wall painting of dolphins owes more to Evans than to the Minoans.

of the Minoan settlements, and occupied Knossos from 1470 to about 1380 B.C. During this period the Mycenaean conquerors replaced Linear A, the native Minoan script, with Linear B.

In 1380 B.C., the palace-complex at Knossos was destroyed by fire. No one knows what caused the fire—perhaps an earthquake, civil unrest, or an invasion by yet another power. From this time on the Mycenaeans shifted their attention away from Crete, although they preserved the legend of King Minos's labyrinth and the Minotaur, which would reappear in the culture of their descendants, the Greeks. The remains of the Minoan civilization were left to await the spades of Arthur Evans and those who came after him.

Knossos today is a reflection as much of Arthur Evans's passion and imagination as of its original Minoan builders. All modern archaeologists who work at sites that have been under excavation for a long time must deal with two different pasts. One past is the distant past, in which the people who built the site lived and worked and died. The other past that modern-day archaeologists must consider is more recent—the history of their predecessors at the site. While archaeologists are trying to learn more about the site and its builders and inhabitants, they must also pay close attention to the history of work at the site, consulting old records, drawings, and photographs, if possible, to see how the work of previous generations of archaeologists has affected the original site. Because each new generation of specialists has tools and methods unknown to prior generations, one of the underlying themes of archaeology is the difficulty of working in sites that have been "contaminated" by earlier investigators.

Knossos is a classic example of site contamination. Arthur Evans wanted to do more than simply uncover and study the ruins of Minoan civilization; he wanted to restore them, as closely as possible, to their original appearance. He hired artists to repaint faded and broken frescoes in bright colors, he shored up stairways with iron girders and concrete, and he rebuilt some of the rooms according to his idea of how they had looked in their prime. The magic that Knossos held for Evans appears in his account of how he stood one moonlit night and gazed at the staircase he had rebuilt, imagining that his favorite figures from the repainted frescoes were moving about: "The whole place seemed to waken a while to life . . . the Priest-King with his plumed lily crown, great ladies, tightly girdled, flounced and corseted, long-stoled priests, and, after them, a retinue of elegant but sinewy youths—as if the Cup-Bearer and his fellows had stepped down from the walls—passed and repassed on the flights below."

However magical, Evans's restoration of Knossos—called "concrete Crete" by some critics—was a mixed blessing. On one hand, archaeologists today have found that some of his reconstructions were simply wrong; from their point of view, the site would be in better shape if he had not attempted to repair it. On the other hand, tens of thousands of visitors have toured the restored palace of Knossos, marveling at the airy rooms with their graceful pillars and lively wall paintings, and Evans's restorations have inspired a great deal of interest in and admiration for the Minoans. Like Schliemann's great trench at Troy, Evans's restorations at Knossos are now part of the history of the site, a modern chapter in a story that began thousands of years ago.

CHAPTER 10

Gournia
A Woman on Muleback

During the exciting decades when one lost city after another was added to the map, archaeology was men's work. Once in a while, in the early days of archaeology, a discoverer's sister or wife—such as Heinrich Schliemann's Sophia—might accompany him to the scene of his triumphs. But the adventurers who searched for buried cities under desert sands or in the green depths of tropical jungles were men. Those who found something interesting became popular heroes. Was there a place in archaeology, women wondered, for heroines?

During the 19th century, most women had little or no chance to act independently or to pursue daring dreams. Even in that repressive time, however, a few bold spirits answered the call of archaeology. One of the first European women to gain wide recognition for her contributions to the new science was Amelia Edwards.

Born in 1831 in England, Edwards traveled frequently in Europe. In 1873, she wrote a popular book about her rambles through the Dolomite Mountains of northern Italy. The following year she was again touring Europe when a long spell of

Tools and everyday objects such as this bowl were among the items found in the buried ruins of Gournia, a Minoan town in eastern Crete that was the first lost city discovered by a woman.

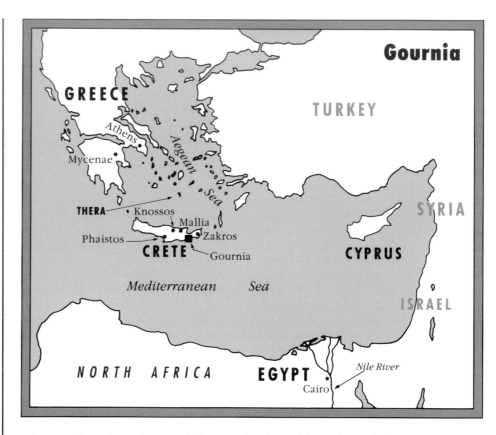

rainy weather drove her south in search of sunshine. She ended up in Egypt—a place she had never planned to visit—and at once fell under the spell of what she later called "the fascination of Egyptian travel, the charm of the Nile, the unexpected and surpassing beauty of the desert, and the ruins which are the wonder of the world."

Edwards explored the city of Cairo and then hired a boat and a crew for a long, leisurely journey up the Nile. She was no idle pleasure traveler, however: Diligently she sketched and measured scores of monuments, temples, and other ruins, compiling an archaeological survey of all that she saw. Her account of the trip, published in 1877 under the title *A Thousand Miles up the Nile,* is not only a lively travel tale, but also a work of serious scholarship, admired by many top archaeologists of Edwards's day. Edwards's connection with Egypt did not end with the publication of her book, which added to the growing interest in Egypt among both ordinary readers and archaeologists. She helped establish Britain's first university position in Egyptology, a science that she had helped to define. Edwards continued her own studies, publishing another book on Egypt in 1891, and by the time of her death a year later was regarded as a leading Egyptologist.

Agnes and Margaret Smith, twin sisters born in 1843 in Scotland, were also intrepid travelers who contributed to the young science of biblical archaeology, although their work concerned ancient documents rather than lost cities. Interested in travel and in languages from an early age, both sisters married scholars. By 1891, both were widowed. The next year they embarked together on a journey to Egypt to visit Mt. Sinai, which Margaret called "the scene of one of the most astonishing miracles recorded in Bible history." According to the Bible, Moses had received the Ten Commandments on the slopes of Mt. Sinai.

At the foot of Mt. Sinai is a very old Christian monastery called St. Catherine's Convent. Before their marriage, Margaret's husband had visited the monastery and seen that its library was full of ancient, long-unread manuscripts. The sisters agreed to photograph one of these manuscripts as a favor for a scholarly friend. That favor led to a remarkable—and utterly accidental—discovery.

While photographing the document their friend had asked about, the sisters noticed a scrap of parchment with two kinds of writing on it: Greek and Syriac. Syriac is the written form of Aramaic, a version of which was spoken by Jesus and his disciples. Eagerly the sisters searched for

The colossal monuments at Abu Simbel on the Nile, from Amelia Edwards's book on Egypt. Edwards helped found the science of Egyptology.

the rest of the Syriac document. They found 358 pages, which turned out to be an early version of the Christian Gospels dating from the 4th century A.D. Known as *Syriac Sinaitis,* the manuscript is of great value both to biblical scholars and to historians studying the ancient Christian world.

Their discovery of the Gospel text made Agnes Smith Lewis and Margaret Smith Gibson famous for a time. The two women continued to travel to St. Catherine's and to other monasteries in Egypt and Lebanon, publishing many translations of old Syriac and Arabic texts. Margaret died in 1920, Agnes in 1926. By that time, women had begun to make a greater mark on the worlds of scholarship and archaeology. One woman had even found a lost city.

Harriet Boyd displays pieces of broken Minoan bowls, jars, and vases in 1902. Two years later the *New York Times* would report that Boyd's expedition had found several completely new types of pottery at Gournia.

Harriet Boyd was the first woman to lead her own archaeological expedition in the Aegean—a region that made headlines around the world when Heinrich Schliemann excavated Troy and Mycenae in the 1870s and Arthur Evans unearthed the palace of Knossos in 1900. Boyd arrived in Crete in 1900, mere days after Evans's discoveries began. She was one of many eager explorers who swarmed across the island, hoping to find more traces of the ancient Minoans.

Born in 1871 in Boston, Massachusetts, Harriet Boyd had been interested in politics and history from an early age. She loved geography and taught herself to draw accurate maps. While Boyd was a student at Smith College in Northampton, Massachusetts, she attended a lecture by Amelia Edwards, author of *A Thousand Miles up the Nile.* According to a 1992 biography of Boyd by her daughter, Mary Allsebrook, Edwards's lecture sparked Boyd's lasting interest in the ancient world and in archaeology. After graduating from Smith, Boyd toured Europe with several classmates and then decided to study ancient Greek history and literature at the American School of Classical Studies in Athens, Greece.

Boyd arrived in Greece in 1896. She visited Mycenae, marveling at the city's huge stone gateway and its ruined palaces, temples, and tombs. She met Sophia Schliemann, who shared anecdotes about her husband's discoveries at Troy and Mycenae, and she accompanied Wilhelm Dorpfeld, who had taken over the task of excavating Troy from Schliemann, on his lecture tours of the ancient temples of Athens. Boyd's studies were interrupted by the outbreak of war between Greece and Turkey in 1897. She joined the corps of Greek and foreign women who volunteered to serve as Red Cross nurses. At several field hospitals near the enemy lines she tended Greek soldiers, both battle casualties and victims of the typhoid epidemic that swept through Greece that year.

As a student at Smith College, Harriet Boyd (holding dog), was drawn to the study of the ancient world after hearing a lecture by explorer and Egyptologist Amelia Edwards. Boyd became the first woman to lead her own archaeological expedition in the Aegean.

Boyd resumed her studies in 1898. She realized, however, that she was not "cut out for a library student," as she put it in a letter. She wanted to excavate a site of her own, perhaps in Crete—"but the field," as her daughter later wrote, "was thought no place for a woman." Undaunted, in early 1900 Boyd sought advice from Arthur Evans, who was passing through Athens on his way to Knossos. Evans's response to Boyd's inquiries was encouraging, so she applied to the Archaeological Institute of America, which agreed to fund a modest expedition. Soon the archaeological community in Athens was buzzing with news of Harriet Boyd's daring plan.

With an American friend named Jean Patten, Boyd arrived in Canea, the capital of Crete, in April 1900. She visited Evans at Knossos and watched breathlessly as his workmen removed the last earth from the stone chair that Evans believed had been the throne of King Minos himself—"the oldest throne in Europe," as Boyd called it. She also met the German archaeologist Federico Halbherr, who was prospecting around the island, looking for a promising site to excavate. Within a few months Halbherr would find the Minoan palace-

Boyd (on horse) and her party return to their camp after a hard day of digging. She faced the inconveniences of rural Cretan life with good humor and even politely ate a sheep's eye—a great delicacy—at the home of a local bishop.

complex at Phaistos, on Crete's south coast.

Boyd, too, was prospecting. She rode around the island on muleback, perched on an uncomfortable wooden saddle, listening to peasants' tales and examining mounds, hoping for a clue that would point the way to a new discovery. She loved what she called "the happy-go-lucky sensation of riding into a village at nightfall, not knowing where you are going to put up."

Finally Boyd settled at Kavousi, a village on the shore of Mirabello Bay, a deep indentation in the northeastern coast of Crete. The local people brought her fragments of pottery found in their fields and told her about other artifacts that had turned up in the area. Some Roman ruins had already been identified near Kavousi, but Boyd was hoping for something dating back much earlier. She hired workmen and bought "20 pickaxes, 20 spades, 50 baskets, 10 large knives and plenty of rope." Then she began excavating high on a nearby hill where she had seen traces of old stone walls. Soon her team had uncovered an Iron Age chieftain's tomb containing a gold button, iron swords, several vases, and a bronze plate engraved with sphinxes and lions. A few more tombs followed.

Time was running short, however. Most archaeological expeditions spend only a few months at a time in the field, during the time of year most favorable for outdoor work—in Crete, the summer. Archaeologists spend the rest of the year teaching, lecturing, raising funds, or writing up their field notes, then return to their site for another season of field work. At the end of their first season in Crete, Boyd and Patten climbed aboard their mules to begin the journey home. Boyd planned to resume her excavations at Kavousi the following year. She hoped to find not just more tombs, but a Minoan settlement.

Boyd returned to Kavousi in 1901. Other archaeologists working on Crete felt sorry for her; they did not believe that Mirabello Bay offered any very exciting possibilities. Perhaps Boyd would find some additional Iron Age relics, but Minoan ruins did not seem likely. Boyd hoped to prove them wrong.

After several weeks spent guiding their surefooted mules up and down narrow mountain tracks around Mirabello Bay, Boyd began to wonder whether there really was anything to find. Then a peasant told her of a spot not far from Kavousi where he had seen some ruins. He showed her a carved sealstone that he had found there. Boyd's interest returned with a rush; she knew that sealstones had led Arthur Evans to his great find at Knossos.

The peasant led Boyd to a small cove called Gournia. There, not far from a modern road, she found bits of broken pottery and traces of stone walls. She brought a crew of 36 Cretan workers from Kavousi and set them to work on the new site. On the first day they found a bronze knife, a spearpoint, and many pieces of vases. But to Boyd the most exciting find was a stretch of well-paved road. No isolated homestead or burial site would have such a road, Boyd reasoned. There must be a city or large town buried at Gournia.

Three days later, Boyd's workers had found a number of houses and roads. She sent a telegram to the American Exploration Society, telling the world that she had found a Minoan settlement. Other searchers were astonished—many of them had traveled along that modern road, passing close to the site of Gournia without ever suspecting it existed. David Hogarth, director of the British School of Archaeology in Athens, visited Boyd at Gournia and described the site for readers of the 10 August 1901 London *Times*:

> . . . the most perfect example yet discovered of a small "Mycenaean" town . . . and at this moment after the two great palaces, is the "sight" best worth visiting in Crete. . . . Unobserved till now, though close to the main road, it was discovered

by the perseverance of the American lady, Miss Harriet Boyd, who has been directing its excavation.

Boyd continued her work at Gournia in 1903 and 1904. By the end of her 1904 season, she had revealed a town that had once covered several acres around a low hill. At the top of the hill was Gournia's largest building, about 12 times larger than the rest of the houses in the community. Boyd dubbed this building the palace; other archaeologists sometimes call it the governor's house. Although no one knows how Gournia's political life was organized, the hilltop building was clearly the residence of the most important people in town. Ranging from one to three stories in height, with a cluster of small rooms and several very large state chambers, the Gournia palace appeared to Boyd to be a small-scale version of the great Minoan palace-complexes of Knossos and Phaistos. She noted that its flat rooftops commanded a stunning view of Mirabello Bay and the cliffs around the bay, and that the men's quarters contained a bath.

North of the palace, on the very top of the hill, Boyd and her crew uncovered a one-room shrine. It was the first Minoan religious sanctuary to be discovered intact, for it had apparently not been looted, as the palace had been. Inside the sanctuary were a statue of a goddess or priestess entwined with snakes, a low altar or table, and several vases.

The palace and shrine were surrounded by a road, well paved with stones, that ringed the top of the hill. Another road circled the lower part of the town east of the hill. Cross streets, very narrow and sometimes including stairways, connected the two main roads. Along these streets were crowded the homes and shops of the ordinary people of Gournia.

Gournia offered a very different view of the Minoans than that presented by Evans's great find and the other palace-complexes, for Gournia was a small town, probably almost self-sufficient. The houses were small, with five or six small rooms on the ground floor; many had upper floors or rooftop terraces. Unlike the grand palace-complexes, which were made of stone that had been finished into smooth blocks, the buildings at Gournia were built of unfinished field stones. However, Boyd found traces of ancient plaster, suggesting that the

This page from Boyd's field notes includes detailed descriptions of various pieces of pottery found at the site.

Boyd (standing, lower left, in white) and her workers at Gournia in 1904. She set up a democratic system, complete with a Senate of older workers and an Assembly of younger ones, through which they could settle disputes among themselves.

Gournians—like many Mediterranean people today—covered their walls with smooth plaster, white or painted.

Boyd's workmen proudly called the town they were uncovering "an industrial city." Many of the buildings appeared to have been the homes or workshops of craftspeople. Near the palace was a carpenter's house, with five chisels, a saw, and an axe prudently concealed under the floor of a hallway. Overlooking the harbor was the shop of the metalsmith, who had owned a stone mold for making bronze nails and chisels. Other buildings were identified with fishermen, potters, weavers, a shoemaker, and a painter. The diggers found much ancient pottery among the ruins. Most pieces had flowers, seaweed, or shells, painted in red or black on a tan background.

Today archaeologists regard Gournia as the most completely preserved small Minoan town. Modern researchers have determined that Gournia was built after the Minoan Old Palace period ended in 1700 B.C. The town was destroyed in the cataclysm that helped to end Minoan civilization in 1470 B.C. It was then partly rebuilt and reoccupied for a few years by Crete's Mycenaean conquerors.

Boyd's team also found traces of an older Minoan settlement at Vasiliki, two miles from Gournia. Vasiliki is thought to date from about 2000 B.C.

When the *New York Times* reported the results of Boyd's third season at Gournia in the fall of 1904, it pointed out that the public was more excited by the sensational news of a lost city than by the patient work of piecing together pottery shards:

> This last campaign is the most important of all in scientific results, although in popular interest it does not rank as high as previous ones. The imagination is stirred more by the discovery of a lost and unknown city . . . than by less spectacular but more significant discoveries.

In 1906, Harriet Boyd married a British scholar and writer, Henry Hawes, and settled in the United States to raise a family. Although she did not return to field archaeology, she wrote a book about Gournia that was described as "a monument of self-denying, scholarly work."

During the first few years of the 20th century, Harriet Boyd gained considerable renown as the first woman to direct her own archaeological expedition— and as the finder of a lost city. In 1902, while she was in the United States between excavation seasons, she crisscrossed the East Coast and the Midwest to lecture about Gournia to 10 local chapters of the Archaeological Institute of America; she was the first woman ever invited to speak to that organization. The London *Times Weekly Edition* said of Boyd, "In these days of woman's emancipation there should be nothing surprising in the successful conduct of a scientific expedition in the Near East by a lady, and least of all by an American lady."

In 1902, the *Philadelphia Public Ledger* summed up Boyd's contributions both to archaeology and to woman's rights: "A woman has shattered another tradition and successfully entered unaided a field hitherto occupied almost exclusively by men, namely archaeological exploration." Other women archaeologists soon moved into that field, among them the Englishwomen Gertrude Bell, who explored ruins in Syria and Iraq, and Gertrude Caton-Thompson, who excavated in Egypt and argued that Great Zimbabwe was of African origin. By the time Boyd died in 1945, women archaeologists were working in field excavations, in laboratories, and in classrooms all around the world.

CHAPTER 11

Machu Picchu

"Behind the Ranges"

By profession, Hiram Bingham was a historian who taught Latin American history at Yale University in Connecticut. But he was no armchair historian, content to read about long-ago times and faraway places. His interest in history was linked to a passion for traveling to the places where history had been made. He took as his motto a verse from Rudyard Kipling's poem "The Explorer":

> Something hidden. Go and find it. Go and
>   look behind the Ranges—
> Something lost behind the Ranges. Lost and
>   waiting for you. Go!

In the early years of the 1900s, Bingham made several arduous field trips. In 1906-07 he crossed the jungles and mountains of Venezuela and Colombia, following the trail once taken by Simón Bolívar, the liberator of South America. Next he followed a centuries-old

Spanish conquistadors melted much Inca treasure, but this silver statue of an alpaca escaped destruction. Machu Picchu is one Inca site that the Spanish never found.

Spanish trade route across the Andes Mountains from Buenos Aires, Argentina, to Lima, Peru. But Bingham's 1911 expedition was to lead the 35-year-old explorer into the most daunting territory he had yet encountered—and further into the past than he had ever gone before.

On July 24, 1911, Bingham was high in the Andes Mountains, northwest of the city of Cuzco, Peru. The landscape was more vertical than horizontal—peaks soared to 18,000 feet on either side of the deep gorges and valleys of the torrential Urubamba River. The road led across steep slopes of slippery rock and tangled vegetation, all wrapped in mist and clouds. The wild beauty of the place captivated Bingham, who wrote:

> In the variety of its charms and the power of its spell, I know of no place in the
> world which can compare with it. Not only has it great snow peaks looming
> above the clouds more than two miles overhead, gigantic precipices of many-
> colored granite rising sheer for thousands of feet above the foaming, glistening,
> roaring rapids; it has also, in striking contrast, orchids and tree ferns, the
> delectable beauty of luxurious vegetation, and the mysterious witchery of the
> jungle.

Bingham and his expedition were searching for Vilcabamba, the last stronghold of the Inca empire, a powerful and accomplished Andean civilization that had been wiped out by Spanish invaders in the 16th century. Cuzco was the traditional Inca capital, but according to Spanish accounts of the last days of the Incas, some 20,000 Incas had fled into the jungle and built a new capital called Vilcabamba. In this remote fastness they managed to hold off the Spanish for a few more years, until Vilcabamba fell in 1572 and the last Inca king was killed. Since that time, Vilcabamba's location had been lost. Hiram Bingham wanted to find it.

The night before, Bingham had heard a local tavernkeeper talk about Inca ruins high on a ridge between two nearby peaks called Huayna Picchu and Machu Picchu. He had persuaded the man to lead him to the ruins. None of the other members of the expedition placed much faith in the tavernkeeper's story, so Bingham set off into the rain with only two companions, the tavernkeeper and a bodyguard assigned by the Peruvian government.

The first challenge was crossing the roaring Urubamba on a precarious, slippery bridge made of a few logs lashed together. The guide and the bodyguard, accustomed to such bridges, walked across barefooted; Bingham, knowing that a plunge into the icy river meant death, crawled across on his hands and knees. Then came the long climb up a steep, wet, snake-infested trail. The tavernkeeper decided to halt at a peasant farmer's hut, but the farmer's 10-year-old son offered to guide Bingham and his bodyguard the rest of the way.

Bingham's excitement mounted as he continued up the mountain. All around were stone terraces, and Bingham figured that these terraces—stone walls that anchored small, flat fields on the steep slopes—had been built by the Incas. Bingham came to the top of the ridge. "Suddenly," he later wrote, "I found myself confronted with the walls of ruined houses built of the finest quality of Inca stonework. It was hard to see them for they were partly covered with trees and

Restless and adventurous by nature, Hiram Bingham became an explorer, his son wrote, to escape the "humdrum life" of a history teacher.

moss, the growth of centuries, but in the dense shadow, hiding in bamboo thickets and tangled vines, appeared here and there walls . . . exquisitely fitted together." The entire saddle between the two craggy peaks was covered with stone ruins: a plaza, large buildings that Bingham took for temples, and many houses. He had come upon the Inca site that today is called Machu Picchu, after one of the mountain peaks that towers over it.

Filled with excitement, Bingham hurried down the mountain and roused his camp. The next day they proceeded to look for other ruins in the area. About 60 miles north of Machu Picchu along the Urubamba River, in an area called Espiritu Pampa (Plain of Ghosts) by the local people, Bingham's expedition located the remains of a much larger Inca city in a jungle lowland. Bingham decided that this second find was the long-lost Inca capital of Vilcabamba.

In 1912, Bingham returned to Machu Picchu to study the mountaintop ruins, and he returned again in 1914–15. After spending some time at Machu Picchu, Bingham reversed his earlier opinion and decided that Machu Picchu, and not the lowland city, was the old capital Vilcabamba. Modern researchers of the history of the Incas, however, have concluded that Bingham's first idea was the correct one: The lowland city was Vilcabamba, and Machu Picchu was an older citadel, outpost, or ceremonial center.

Bingham became famous for his discovery of "the lost city in the clouds," as Machu Picchu was romantically called. Yet like many archaeological sites that have been called lost cities, Machu Picchu was not exactly lost. Although partly overgrown with vegetation, it was visible, not buried under a mound of earth like Troy or Knossos. The people who lived around the mountain were well aware of the existence of the ruins, and some of the local farmers had cleared the trees from the old Inca terraces to plant their own crops of corn, potatoes, beans, and peppers. Machu Picchu had even received a few visitors from the outside world, some of whom had scrawled graffiti on its white granite walls. But Bingham was the first to tell the world at large about the ruins and to conduct a scientific exploration of the site. He remained associated with Machu Picchu even after retiring from active archaeology in 1918; he died in 1956, after writing several books about his travels and serving in the U.S. Senate.

Some rediscovered cities have introduced entire civilizations whose very existence had been unsuspected. Heinrich Schliemann's digs at Troy and Mycenae, for example, brought to light the Mycenaean culture that had once dominated the Aegean Sea, and the discovery of the pueblos at Chaco Canyon introduced the Anasazi of the American Southwest to the historical record.

This was not the case with Machu Picchu and Vilcabamba. Historians of Bingham's day knew a great deal about the Incas from Spanish chronicles written at the time of the Spanish invasion and in the decades that followed, when Europeans subdued the Inca empire and made it one of their colonies. More recent studies have added much to our knowledge of this mountain culture.

The Incas arose as a recognizable culture in the Cuzco valley around A.D. 1200. They remained in this homeland until, in 1438, a king named Yupanqui came to power. He took the royal name Pachacuti, which means "Earthshaker," and he certainly shook up the Incas. During Pachacuti's rule, in a swift surge of empire-building, the Incas conquered or absorbed a host of other peoples up and down the spine of the Andes. Pachacuti proved to be not just a conqueror but a brilliant administrator. He developed a system of government that welded a patchwork of peoples into a unified empire.

One hundred years after Pachacuti became king, at about the time the Spanish arrived, the Inca aristocracy ruled an empire that they called Tahuantinsuyu (Land of the Four Quarters). The empire stretched from the modern nation of Colombia in the north for 2,500 miles south along the Andes Mountains to the present-day site of Santiago, Chile. In the east it reached to the edge of the great low-lying rainforests of Brazil; in the west it was bordered by the Atacama Desert,

Like many dwellers in mountainous countries, the Incas built terraces to create fields and gardens on steep slopes. After the Incas left Machu Picchu, local Indians continued to farm these terraces. Hiram Bingham found several flourishing farms there when he "discovered" Machu Picchu.

which runs along South America's western coast. The Incas' subjects numbered 9 million people belonging to 100 different ethnic groups.

Policies established by Pachacuti unified this far-flung empire. The Inca rulers kept unrest among their conquered subjects to a minimum by allowing the subjects to retain their own rulers and gods, although the native rulers were subject to Inca authority and the conquered peoples had to add worship of the Inca sun god to their native religions. Another important unifying factor was language. The Incas' subject peoples could continue to speak their native languages, but everyone in the empire also had to learn Quechua, the Inca language. According to one Spanish chronicler, this rule "was so strictly enforced that an infant had not yet left its mother's breast before they began to teach it the language it had to know." It is a mark of the Incas' widespread and long-lasting influence that Quechua is still spoken today by 10 million people in the highlands of Peru, Bolivia, and Ecuador.

Inca society was highly structured and organized into classes. At the top was the emperor, called the Sapa Inca. The Sapa Inca was regarded as a descendant of Inti, the sun god, who was the Incas' supreme deity. A Sapa Inca could have hundreds of concubines, or secondary wives, but only one empress, who was called the Coya. The Sapa Inca always chose one of his sisters for his Coya. Among the Incas, as among the Egyptians and some other ancient peoples, the royal bloodline was considered semidivine. Royal marriages between siblings ensured that the heirs to the empire would come from this bloodline.

The Coya was an independent and powerful figure. She maintained her own court and frequently played a role in imperial politics and administration. The highest-ranking nobles in the empire were the Capac Incas, members of the original hereditary aristocracy of the Inca people. The Capac Incas probably numbered no more than a few thousand, but they were extremely powerful. Together with the Sapa Inca, they controlled the land and resources of the empire: gold, silver, cloth, handicrafts, and other goods were all the property of the nobility. Capac Inca women possessed a high degree of independence. They inherited privileges—such as the right to claim a share of labor or resources from the peasants—from their mothers, while Capac Inca men inherited their status and privileges from their fathers. Scholars have coined the terms *split inheritance* and *parallel inheritance* to describe this system of inheritance by gender.

Below the Capac Incas were the Hahua Incas, people promoted to noble status by the emperor as a reward for their services; some of them came from the humble ranks of society. Below the Hahua Incas were the *curacas,* local rulers of native peoples who had become officials in the Inca government when the Incas absorbed their states. The *curacas* shared some of the privileges of the nobility: They could have more than one wife, ride in litters, and eat from gold or silver dishes.

The government to which the *curacas* belonged was centralized and highly organized, with a large bureaucracy of officials who oversaw most details of everyday life. The entire population of the empire was divided into units. The smallest unit was 10 households; the largest, 10,000 households. Each of these units had an administrator who was responsible to the regional governor and, ultimately, to the emperor. The administrators told people when to work, what to plant, and when to gather for festivals, ceremonies, or public projects such as building temples. Scholars estimate that nearly one-third of every year was devoted to religious rituals, public gatherings, and other state events. In return for such a high degree of control over people's lives, the state provided everyone with a job and, during hard times, with food and other goods from the public storehouses.

Money did not exist in the Inca empire, and neither did private property. All land belonged to the emperor and the aristocracy. Speaking of the peasants who made up the great majority of the empire's population, a Spanish chronicler named Juan Polo de Ondegardo wrote, "Not a foot of land was theirs, but every year they were allotted land to be sown." Before peasants could work in the fields set aside for their families, however, they had to put in a specified number of hours tending crops for the Sapa Inca and the priesthood. Every household in the empire paid taxes in the form of labor and a share of crops or other goods produced. One labor tax was called the *mita*, or "turn," in which each household owed a stint of labor in the army, the gold and silver mines, the road-building crews, or some other state-operated activity. Craftspeople paid taxes, too. The nobility provided them with raw materials such as gold, clay, and cloth, and the artisans paid their taxes with finished artifacts such as jewelry, pottery, and clothing. Weaving was perhaps the most highly honored craft. The finest, most magnificently decorated cloth was reserved for the clothing of the nobles and the Sapa Inca. A single embroidered royal tunic could take hundreds of hours to weave and contain 10 miles of yarn in dozens of complex patterns.

To help administrators keep tabs on the provinces, the Incas built one of the world's most efficient transportation networks: more than 15,000 miles of stone roads that linked all parts of their empire, with regularly spaced way stations where travelers could eat and sleep. Specially trained runners carried messages along these highways, sometimes covering a hundred miles or more in a day. Although the Incas did not develop writing, they created their own form of recordkeeping using knotted cords called *quipus*. Few *quipus* survive today—most were burned by Spanish monks, who called them "the devil's work"—and researchers have not fully decoded their complex systems of colors and knots. We know from the Spanish chronicles, however, that the *quipus* were counting tools. Specially trained *quipu*-makers were the Incas' accountants or statisticians, who kept track of resources, population, and taxes paid and owed.

Religion was a government-sponsored affair in the Inca empire. The religious hierarchy of the empire resembled its civil government, with a head priest in charge of bishops, who were all Inca nobles. The bishops in turn oversaw thousands of priests and priestesses throughout the provinces.

One of the most sacred duties of the priesthood was preserving royal corpses as mummies. Many Andean peoples, including some who had lived long before the Incas, had developed the custom of mummifying their dead. The Incas believed that a person who died would enjoy an eternal afterlife—as long as his or her body was preserved unharmed. Inca embalmers perfected mummification

techniques that are still not fully understood by modern scientists. The chronicler Garcilaso de la Vega, the son of an Inca princess and a Spanish soldier, saw several royal mummies, including that of Pachacuti himself, and reported that "not a hair, not an eyebrow, not even a lash was missing."

By the time of the Spanish invasion, reverence for the royal mummies had grown into a cult of mummy worship. Servants dressed and tended the mummies, attendants carried the mummies through the capital city of Cuzco in elaborate processions, and worshippers among the nobility asked their advice on matters of state. Many of the royal Inca mummies, including that of the Earthshaker, were destroyed by the Spanish. Since the 1960s, however, archaeologists have located a number of mummies belonging to the Incas and other Andean cultures. Some of these mummies may have been hidden hundreds of years ago to prevent them from falling into Spanish hands.

"Would anyone believe what I had found?" wrote Bingham in *Lost City of the Incas.* His books and photographs drew the world's attention to the "city in the clouds." Machu Picchu is now Peru's most popular tourist site.

The Incas worshipped many gods and goddesses, each of whom had special temples, altars, and ceremonies. The creator was called Viracocha; lesser deities included Pachamama, the earth mother, and Illapa, the thunder god. Most important to the Inca aristocracy was Inti, the sun god, from whom the Incas believed themselves to be descended. Gold and silver, which the Incas possessed in plenty, were called "the sweat of the sun" and "the tears of the moon." Craftspeople used these metals—along with emeralds, jade, and shells—to make jewelry, statues, and other objects for royal or religious use. Garcilaso de la Vega told of golden ornaments in the Sapa Inca's gardens: "birds set in the trees, as though

A depiction of Francisco Pizzaro's arrival on the coast of Peru in 1532. Forty years later, the Spanish had killed the last emperor of the Incas and destroyed their last fortress.

they were about to sing, and others bent over the flowers, breathing in their nectar." One Spanish conquistador described a massive gold fountain, with gold in the likeness of water spraying from it. The Spanish melted these and countless other works of art into ingots.

Although the Incas excelled at controlling their subject peoples, they fell victim to a split within their own ranks. On the eve of the Spanish invasion the Inca empire was torn apart by civil war when two princes, Atahualpa and Huascar, vied for supremacy. The Incas formed factions, and bloody fighting began. Just at this time, when the Incas were divided and weak, the conquistador Francisco Pizarro and his small but ruthless band of Spanish adventurers arrived in 1532, set on plundering the Inca gold. Cleverly taking advantage of the disarray in the empire, the Spanish killed Atahualpa, who had taken the throne. The conquest of the Incas proceeded swiftly from that point. By 1572, the Spanish had destroyed the Incas' last fortress at Vilcabamba and killed their last emperor, Tupac Amaru.

Machu Picchu, the site found by Hiram Bingham in 1911, has now been extensively excavated and studied. Experts today think that Machu Picchu was not a city in the common sense of the term but rather a center for religious rites, possibly built by the Earthshaker, Pachacuti. The 200 buildings at Machu Picchu include many temples and food-storage vaults. Perhaps as many as 1,200 people lived in Machu Picchu, farming the terraces and tending the temples and altars, but larger crowds may have converged on the site at intervals for festivals or rituals.

The center of Machu Picchu is a long open space that archaeologists have named the Sacred Plaza. Here, experts believe, ceremonies took place, perhaps in honor of the sun god. A stairway leads from the Sacred Plaza up a steep stone outcropping that overlooks the plaza. On a platform atop this outcropping is an *intihuatana,* a sacred rock whose name means "hitching post of the sun." Other *intihuatanas* have been found throughout the former Inca empire, but the one at Machu Picchu is the largest known today. Unlike the temples and other buildings at the site, it is not built of stone masonry; it is carved from the solid bedrock of the mountain. Scholars suggest that Inca priests used the stone as an observatory, marking seasons and holidays by observing the stone's shadow. The *intihuatana* may also have been the site of special ceremonies at the winter and summer solstices in June and December.

Machu Picchu is just one of hundreds of Inca fortresses, cities, and strongholds dotted throughout the former empire. Yet Machu Picchu has always had a special fascination for the world. Today it is Peru's leading tourist attraction, despite the fact that it lies in a region troubled by political terrorism since the 1970s.

Part of the glamour of Machu Picchu comes from the exciting story of its discovery by a historian who—like filmmaker Steven Spielberg's dashing hero Indiana Jones—was also a slouch-hatted, khaki-jacketed adventurer. And part of the glamour comes from Machu Picchu's setting, high in the clouds between two green, forbidding peaks. Machu Picchu seems to have been abandoned by its builders around the time of the Spanish invasion, perhaps earlier. The Spanish never plundered Machu Picchu or even discovered it; the Spanish chroniclers can tell us nothing about the sacred retreat or the role it played in Inca life. Wrapped in mystery and cloud, Machu Picchu stands today as a marvel of mountaintop engineering and a monument to one of the largest empires the world has ever known.

CHAPTER 12

Ur
Back to the Beginning

A rchaeologists love graves. They have learned that the way in which people buried their dead can tell us a great deal about how those people lived. Burying the dead with rituals and artifacts is apparently a very old human custom. Archaeologists have found prehistoric graves in which traces of paint or flowers show us that the dead were interred with ceremony thousands of years before people began farming or living in cities.

Many of the civilizations that have arisen in various parts of the world have followed elaborate burial practices that were probably intended to help the dead make a smooth journey to the afterlife. A dead person, especially a royal or noble dead person, would be buried with a great store of goods. These grave goods, ranging from stately treasures and splendid artworks to everyday items such as combs and bowls, are troves of information for modern archaeologists. For this reason the discovery of a

The kings and queens of Ur, one of the world's oldest cities, went to their graves accompanied by royal treasures, such as this statue of a ram rearing up to eat a bush.

burial site is one of the most exciting things that can happen at any archaeological dig.

The British archaeologist C. (later Sir) Leonard Woolley (1880–1960) did not know what to expect when he began digging into a large mound in southern Iraq in 1922. The 60-foot-tall mound was located 12 miles from the Euphrates River in southern Iraq, a region already known to be rich in relics of early history. Called Mesopotamia by historians, this area was the fertile home of many ancient civilizations. Travelers and archaeologists had been probing Mesopotamia's mysteries since the middle of the 19th century. The mound that Woolley was preparing to study had been visited nearly 70 years earlier, in 1854, by J. E. Taylor, a British diplomatic official. Burrowing into the mound, Taylor found some small clay cylinders carved with cuneiform (wedge-shaped) symbols, a form of writing known to have originated in Mesopotamia. The cylinders were what archaeologists call foundation deposits. They had been buried at the corner of a building to record the work of a Babylonian king. Henry Creswicke Rawlinson, a British expert on cuneiform who had helped to decode the symbols, read the royal cylinders that Taylor found. Rawlinson determined that the mound was the site of Ur, an ancient city mentioned in the Bible's Book of Genesis as the birthplace of Abraham, patriarch of the Jews.

After Taylor's visit, Ur received sporadic attention from archaeologists, but not until Woolley's expedition of 1922 was it the target of a large-scale, systematic excavation. Unlike Taylor and many other 19th-century antiquarians, Woolley was not a lone enthusiast poking about the site. Woolley helped make archaeology a group endeavor, a coordinated search for knowledge. He was the director of a well-organized field expedition supported by the British Museum and the University of Pennsylvania. Instead of searching for impressive or valuable finds, he and his colleagues would use the principles of scientific archaeology that had been developed during the early years of the 20th century. Among these were stratigraphy, or the dating of artifacts by the level at which they were buried, and plotting, in which the site is overlaid by a set of lines forming a grid so that the location of every find can be recorded precisely on the framework of the grid.

"Our object was to get history, not to fill museum cases with miscellaneous curios," said Woolley of this new approach to archaeology. He practiced what he preached, closely supervising the local workmen he hired as diggers and making sure that work at the site proceeded slowly and methodically. Yet this patient approach was far from dull. Earlier excavations at Ur had revealed something of the city as it looked during the 6th century B.C., when it was part of the kingdom of Babylon. Now Woolley intended to peel back the layers of time and see what Ur had looked like even earlier. The workmen began deepening an existing trench, and, as Woolley later reported, "at once things began to happen."

The excavators came upon clay and stone jars, bronze tools, and beads. Some of the beads were gold; others were made of a reddish stone called carnelian and a deep blue stone called lapis lazuli. These items were highly prized in ancient Mesopotamia, for they came from far away, along trade routes from Iran and Afghanistan. When he saw the beads, Woolley knew that he had uncovered an important site. Very likely the beads and other objects were grave goods, and he had found an ancient cemetery.

Many archaeologists would perhaps have tackled the cemetery without an instant's hesitation—the name of Heinrich Schliemann, discoverer of treasure

Leonard Woolley removes a buried figurine from a grave at Ur. Woolley developed new methods of excavating fragile, decayed, or broken artifacts.

at Troy and Mycenae, springs to mind. But Woolley was determined to do things right. He knew that the excavation of the cemetery would produce a richer harvest of knowledge if both the archaeologists and the local workers possessed more experience. In addition, he feared that the discovery of treasure would cause trouble at the site. So for four years, Woolley postponed work on the cemetery. During that time he trained his workers in the most delicate and careful excavation techniques, teaching them to use small hand tools, brushes, and even dental picks to remove the earth from around buried objects so that the artifacts could be studied in place. To preserve objects exactly as they were found, Woolley developed a method of pouring hot wax over them, letting it cool, and then lifting the wax and the objects from the ground in a solid mass. In this way a collection of jumbled artifacts—broken pottery, beads from a necklace whose string had rotted away, splintered bits of a metal or wooden box or a delicate and priceless musical instrument—could be held together in their original relationship for restoration and further study.

Woolley wanted to date the cemetery accurately, but he knew that this could not be done until he had established a complete chronology of Ur. From 1922 to 1927, he and his colleagues patiently examined layer after layer of the site, working their way down to the first evidences of habitation. By the end of this time they had developed a timetable. Ur had originated as a settlement of prehistoric farmers on the banks of the Euphrates River around 5500 B.C. By 4000 B.C., it was established as one of the cities of a people that modern scholars call the Sumerians, after Sumer, the ancient name for the region in southern Iraq where the Tigris and Euphrates Rivers meet. Ur passed through many different phases, belonging in turn to the Sumerian, Babylonian, Assyrian, Neo-Babylonian, and Persian empires of the ancient Middle East. Each of these phases was reflected in a layer of remains at the site. Ur's story ended at about 400 B.C., when the Euphrates shifted its course and left the city high and dry. Abandoned by its citizens, Ur was gradually covered over with windblown earth.

Woolley's years of preparation were eventful. During them, the archaeologists uncovered the ziggurat of Ur, an immense artificial mountain like the pyramids of Egypt and the Maya pyramids of Central America. Made of millions of bricks of baked clay, the ziggurat was built around 2000 B.C. by a Sumerian king named Ur-Nammu. This king carried out an ambitious program of building projects throughout Sumer, which consisted of Ur and a number of other cities. In addition to city walls, irrigation canals, and temples, Ur-Nammu constructed many ziggurats, which were believed to create connections between the earthly world and the gods. The ziggurat at Ur was the largest of these structures, reaching a height of 80 feet. In the centuries after Ur-Nammu, the ziggurat was rebuilt at least seven times.

During the 1920s, Woolley's dig at Ur became a stopping point for many travelers in Mesopotamia. One distinguished visitor was the mystery novelist Agatha Christie, who later used both Mesopotamia and archaeology in several of her mysteries. Christie, who had married one of Woolley's colleagues on the dig, described the appeal of archaeology in her autobiography:

> I fell in love with Ur, with its beauty in the evenings, the ziggurat standing up, faintly shadowed, and that wide sea of sand with its lovely pale colours of apricot, rose, blue and mauve, changing every minute. I enjoyed the workmen, the foremen, the little basket boys, the pick men—the whole technique and life. The lure of the past came up to grab me. To see a dagger slowly appearing, with its gold glint, through the sand was romantic. The carefulness of lifting pots and objects from the soil filled me with a longing to be an archaeologist myself.

Finally, in 1927, Woolley and his team were ready to begin work on the cemetery. They soon realized that it was one of the most important finds ever made in Mesopotamia. Parts of the cemetery dated from the height of Sumerian civilization, around 2500 B.C. There were two kinds of graves: rectangular shafts and vaulted chambers. The simple shafts, Woolley determined, were the graves of ordinary people, but the stone or brick chambers were royal tombs. Woolley

excavated the cemetery until 1931, unearthing a total of 1,850 graves. Of these, 16 were royal tombs. But to Woolley's dismay, all but two of the tombs had been plundered by grave-robbers thousands of years earlier, perhaps not long after the burials had taken place. It was clear that these tombs had once contained a treasure in grave goods; the robbers had left behind scraps of gold, scattered beads, and a few overlooked items, such as a silver model of a boat and a gold dagger with a lapis lazuli handle.

Two of the royal tombs remained undisturbed, though, and they yielded grave goods of extraordinary richness and beauty. An ancient queen had gone to her grave adorned with combs, ear-

Woolley (bottom, second from left) assembled a huge crew of workmen to excavate Ur. Their work proceeded slowly and methodically, using the principles of scientific archaeology.

rings, rings, and a headdress of beautifully worked gold. A king's tomb contained such artifacts as harps covered with gold foil. Statues, bowls and jars, and even pieces of furniture, all adorned with gold and lapis, gave glimpses of the majesty of court life in Sumer. Yet these grave goods, stunning though they are, were not the most remarkable features of the graves of Ur.

Outside each of the royal tombs was a shaft that Woolley called a death pit, and in these pits were scores of skeletons, both male and female. Clothing and ornaments indicated that the bodies had belonged to many ranks, from servants up to noble or even royal households. The skeletons showed no sign of violence or disturbance—even the feather-delicate headdresses of the women were in place, suggesting that the victims had died without protest. Beside each skeleton was a cup. Woolley speculated that the bodies were those of family members and attendants who had been sacrificed to accompany the dead personage into the afterlife. It is possible that the victims drank poison and then lay on the floor and died. Then the underground graves were closed, sealing in the retinue of sacrificial victims with the master or mistress they had served in life.

The death pits were a moving and awe-inspiring sight. "One of the royal tombs," wrote Woolley, "which contained no less than 74 bodies buried alive at the bottom of the deep royal shaft, appeared, when exposed, to be a golden carpet ornamented with the beech leaf head-dresses of the ladies of the court, and overlaid by gold and silver harps and lyres which had played the funeral dirge to the end." Macabre as such mass sacrifices appear today, archaeologists believe that court members willingly committed suicide, accepting it as their duty—or perhaps their privilege—to accompany their kings and queens into the afterlife.

Woolley's work at Ur ended in 1934, when he moved on to excavate sites in Turkey. His work and that of many other archaeologists in Mesopotamia brought the Sumerian civilization to light. The first known builders of cities and users of the wheel, of written language, and of the calendar, the Sumerians passed their cultural legacy on to the many peoples who succeeded them in Mesopotamia, often called "the cradle of civilization."

Civilization arose in Sumer at a time of climate change there. Modern geologists and climatologists who have thoroughly studied the Persian Gulf region—in some cases as part of the search for oil—have created a climate map of the region that goes back 20,000 years, to the last Ice Age. At that time, so much of the earth's water was locked up in great continental ice sheets that the Persian Gulf was dry. By 12,000 B.C. the ice was melting, the world's seas were rising, and water was entering the gulf. By 4000 B.C., the Persian Gulf was even bigger

A wooden panel decorated with stones and shells shows the king at a banquet (top row, left); below, servants bring livestock and other goods. Found in the royal tombs at Ur, the panel dates from about 2500 B.C. It is part of an artifact that scholars call the Royal Standard of Ur, although its original use is unknown.

than it is today. The northern end of the Gulf covered land where today the Tigris and Euphrates Rivers flow through a low-lying delta, and the shoreline of the Gulf was very close to the site of Ur.

Life in early Sumer revolved around water. People fished in the Gulf and in the coastal deltas and swamps that formed as the sea level very slowly fell and the shoreline gradually moved southward. The Sumerians built nimble reed boats by which to navigate their watery world; traces of this waterborne way of life linger today among the marsh-dwelling people of southern Iraq. The Sumerians also learned to control floods with dams and canals, and they mastered the use of irrigation to produce abundant harvests in the semideserts of Mesopotamia. Families and then villages began cooperating to build and maintain ever more elaborate water-control systems. Such cooperation may have formed the basis for the first communal governments, which grew into cities.

Ur was not the first city in Sumer; modern archaeologists think that Uruk, northwest of Ur, was the area's first large population center, with a thousand or more inhabitants by 4800 B.C. By 3000 B.C., Uruk covered 250 acres and housed thousands of people. The earliest-known writing—cuneiform symbols recording details of trade and farm production—appears on clay tablets found in Uruk. They date from about 3300 B.C., perhaps years before the people of Egypt developed their own written language.

While Uruk was growing, other city-states came into being in Sumer: among them were Eridu, Nippur, Lagash, Kish, and Ur. At times they warred with one another, and at other times a single strong king was able to meld them into a unified

kingdom. The Sumerian cities had trade links with Syria, Lebanon, Turkey, Egypt, Afghanistan, and Iran; the Sumerians even established their own colonies in Iran and Syria to provide themselves with such goods as timber and precious stones.

Although they were often rivals, the Sumerian city-states were unified by a shared religion. Sumerians believed that forces such as weather and fertility were controlled by powerful gods and goddesses, and the religious life of Sumer revolved around services intended to win the favor of these deities. The cities contained large and magnificent temples, in which life-sized statues of gods and goddesses were offered food, drink, and other goods. Many of the most important shrines were built atop the ziggurats, or artificial mountains, which were regarded as links between the earthly realm and the divine realm of the heavens.

Kings were believed to receive their power to rule from the gods, and each king was responsible for maintaining and, if possible, improving his city's temples. Craftspeople produced thousands of small figures of the gods and goddesses in clay, stone, and gold; these figures adorned shrines in private houses and public buildings. Chief among the Sumerians' hundreds of deities were An, Enlil, and Enki, creators of heavens, air, and water; Ninhursag, a powerful goddess called "the mother of the gods"; and Inanna, goddess of fertility, sexuality, and war. Inanna later became identified with the Babylonian goddess Ishtar.

Around 2330 B.C., Sumer's warring city-states were unified under a single ruler, Sargon the Great. Sargon was not a Sumerian; he was an Akkadian, a member of a nomadic tribe that had settled in the plains north of Sumer. For centuries the Sumerians and the Akkadians lived in relative harmony. The Akkadians

Archaeologists believe that this panel of beaten copper once decorated the entrance to a temple in Ur. The figures are two stags and an eagle with the head of a lion.

Cuneiform writing on a baked clay tablet records amounts of barley given as loans or payments to temple workmen in 2048 B.C. Such records still have much to reveal about the economic and political life of ancient Ur.

adopted many features of Sumerian culture, including cuneiform writing, although they kept their own language. Sargon came to power in the city of Kish—scholars are not sure how—and swiftly conquered Uruk, Ur, and other cities.

Sargon built a capital that he named Agade and forged an empire that his successors held together for several generations. By 2200 B.C., enemies from Iran, Syria, and Turkey were encroaching on the empire's frontiers, and the Sumerian city-states were restless under Akkadian rule. When Sharkalisharri, Sargon's last successor, died in 2193, the empire collapsed. The city-states threw off their Akkadian governors and returned to Sumerian rule. The Akkadian empire vanished, leaving behind one of archaeology's great mysteries: the location of Sargon's capital. Although archaeologists have found many inscriptions that mention Agade and describe it, no one has yet found the city itself. It lies somewhere under the desert sand, waiting to be discovered.

Because of the work of Leonard Woolley, Ur is today the best-known of all Sumerian archaeological sites. It reached its peak around 2300 B.C., when it covered 250 acres and had two harbors to handle its shipping: one on the Euphrates and the other on a large canal. At the core of the city was a walled area that contained the ziggurat, the largest and most important temples, and the royal palaces. Between this central core and the city's outer defense wall was a busy, crowded community of tightly clustered buildings and narrow walkways. Here groups such as bakers, goldsmiths, and priests each had their own neighborhoods, with shrines, canals for washing, and communal ovens. Woolley loved to take visitors on tours through this part of Ur, pointing out details of the everyday life of common people.

Ur became the capital and most important city of Sumer under Ur-Nammu, the ambitious builder who ordered the construction of Ur's great ziggurat, which was dedicated to the moon god Nanna. Ur-Nammu also created the world's oldest known law code, which, according to the ancient scribe who wrote it down, was designed to "establish equity in the land, banish abuse, violence, and strife."

The glories of Ur, and of Sumer, began to fade a few generations later. Squabbling between royal factions divided the realm, which came under increasing pressure from outside. Warlike peoples called the Elamites, from southern Iran, invaded Sumer and conquered Ur in 2004 B.C. A Sumerian poet lamented the fall of Ur in a poem addressed to the wife of Nanna, the moon god: "Your city has been made into ruins; how can you exist! Your house has been laid bare; how has your heart led you on! Ur, the shrine, has been given over to the wind."

Ur, in fact, was not "given over to the wind"—not just yet. The city remained alive for hundreds of years, as part of the Babylonian and Assyrian empires. Through the Babylonians, the Assyrians, the Persians, and other ancient peoples, elements of Sumerian life such as writing and codes of law survived to become part of the heritage of the modern world.

In recent years, war and political tensions have curtailed archaeological investigation of Ur and Iraq's other Sumerian sites. However, Sumerologists and Assyriologists can still study the enormous number of cuneiform texts that remain to be translated. At the University of Pennsylvania, experts in cuneiform and in computer science have created databases of the Sumerian language and of specific tablets. This wealth of information about the world of the ancient Sumerians is still being explored.

There is a French saying that translates, "The more things change, the more they are the same." One of the most important lessons of archaeology is that the more we learn about the people of bygone eras, the more we realize that they were much like us. A common humanity links the people of today with the citizens of even the oldest lost cities. The clay tablets unearthed at Ur record the thoughts and sayings of people who lived 5,000 years ago—and yet many of them sound as though they had been written yesterday. Some display a wry humor, as in the proverb "Making loans is as easy as making love, but repaying them is as hard as bearing a child." But other inscriptions remind us that thoughts about the passage of time are as old as human civilization itself. In words that might have been addressed to the men and women of today who are dedicated to retrieving the human past from the dust of oblivion, one long-dead Babylonian wrote: "The gods alone live forever under the divine sun; but as for mankind, their days are numbered, and their activities will be nothing but wind."

 Ubar
A Discovery in the Desert

Several thousand years ago, according to legends and old histories, a city called Ubar flourished in the sands of the Arabian Peninsula. Ubar was a center of the caravan trade in frankincense and myrrh, the fragrant tree resins from the south coast of Arabia that were prized throughout the Near East and the Mediterranean world as ingredients in perfumes, incense, medicines, and embalming preparations.

Ubar grew rich on the incense trade. Surpassingly lovely, the city was said to be "an imitation of paradise," with mighty towers and lush orchards—an impressive sight, almost a magical one, in the midst of the bleak desert. An Arab historian named al-Hamdani, writing in the 6th century A.D., called Ubar the finest of Arabia's treasures. But, like the cities of Sodom and Gomorrah in the Bible, Ubar was also said to have been a sinful place. It was so wicked that God destroyed it in a mighty cataclysm, just as Sodom and Gomorrah were destroyed. According to a tale in the *Arabian Nights,* the disaster that destroyed Ubar "blotted out the very roads that led to the city."

But tales of Ubar's riches and greatness swirled through the centuries, keeping the memory of the city alive, although the tales began to seem as much myth as history. Scholars speculated that Ubar was the city that is called Iram in the Koran, the holy book of Islam. The Koran, however, does not tell where Iram was located.

In the early 1980s, researchers used the latest satellite technology to help find the location of Ubar, a city lost and buried for more than a thousand years in the desolate Arabian desert.

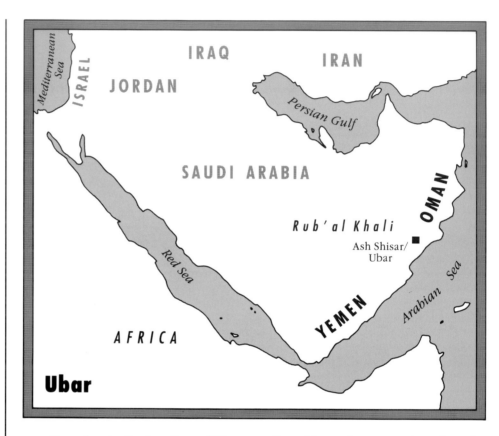

Ubar

One clue to the location of Ubar was found in antique maps based on the work of the Greek geographer Ptolemy, who lived in Egypt in the 2nd century A.D. Ptolemy's maps show a city called Omanum Emporium (Marketplace of Oman) on the Arabian Peninsula, near where the nation of Oman is located today. According to Ptolemy, the people of this region were called Ubarites. Unfortunately, Ptolemy's geography of Arabia was rather distorted. Although his maps suggested that Ubar existed, they did not give a precise location.

More than one attempt has been made in modern times to find Ubar. One who dreamed of discovering the lost city was T. E. Lawrence. A flamboyant British officer who served in Arabia during World War I, Lawrence became known as "Lawrence of Arabia" for his love of Arab culture and his daredevil military exploits. Lawrence compared Ubar to the legendary lost continent supposedly buried beneath the waves somewhere in the Atlantic Ocean, calling Ubar "the Atlantis of the sands." He planned to search the Arabian desert for the site of Ubar, but he left Arabia in 1920 without carrying out his plans. In the 1930s, an Englishman named Bertram Thomas was exploring the Rub'al Khali, or Empty Quarter: a vast district of the Arabian Peninsula that consists of stony wasteland and towering sand dunes and is inhabited only by bands of wandering Bedouin. One day Thomas came across traces of a caravan track that his Bedouin companions said was "the road to Ubar." Nearby was a water hole called Ash Shisar, where Thomas saw the remains of a "rude fort" that appeared to be a few hundred years old. Unimpressed, Thomas moved on.

In the early 1980s, a California filmmaker named Nicholas Clapp, who was researching trade routes in ancient Arabia, read Thomas's reference to the road and the water hole. Clapp was certain that Thomas had stumbled upon Ptolemy's Omanum Emporium and the site of fabled Ubar—but how could Clapp hope to find that site again in the immensity of the Empty Quarter? Technology provided the answer. Clapp read an account of a remote-sensing device called Space Imaging Radar that had been carried on a space shuttle flight in 1981. The high-technology radar system had scanned Egypt from space, and the images it produced showed ancient riverbeds, long dried up and buried under the drifting sands. If the shuttle's radar could reveal buried riverbeds in Egypt, reasoned Clapp, it could find a lost city in Arabia. He called the Jet Propulsion Laboratory in Pasadena, California, which had developed the radar system, and asked, "If a city was buried in the desert, could you see it by this radar?"

Several scientists from the laboratory began working with Clapp and his partner, a lawyer and amateur archaeologist named George Hedges. In 1984, they arranged for the shuttle's radar to scan the segment of the Empty Quarter that Thomas had described. The scan did not reveal any buried cities, but it did show faint traces of old caravan routes. Some of these tracks ran for hundreds of miles across the desert. At times they disappeared beneath huge 600-foot sand dunes and reappeared on the other side, which meant that the tracks had been made hundreds of years ago, before the dunes were formed. The next step was for the researchers to combine the information from the shuttle's Space Imaging Radar with photographs taken by American and French satellites. By photographing large areas in light wavelengths invisible to the human eye, satellite cameras can reveal geological disturbances that would be invisible to observers on the ground—such as sand that was worn into especially fine particles along what were once heavily used caravan routes.

Using computers to enhance and combine the images from the shuttle and the satellites, the researchers produced a map of caravan trails that converged on a region in the southern part of Oman, on the edge of the Empty Quarter. With the support of American and Omani backers, Clapp and Hedges recruited a team of archaeologists and geologists. In 1990, they began exploring the network of trails. During their first year, they ruled out several possible sites for Ubar. In November 1991, they focused their efforts on the well called Ash Shisar, where Thomas had spotted the remains of a fort. Thomas had been right to dismiss the fort as nothing very special, but the new explorers had tools that Thomas had not dreamed of. They used ground-penetrating radar to peer beneath the earth's surface. Hidden under the sands, they found the ruins of a lost city.

Excavations at the site revealed an eight-sided fortress or castle with eight towers, each of which may once have been 30 feet tall. The fortress probably housed no more than 150 people, but hundreds, perhaps thousands, of people may have lived nearby in tents or outlying settlements yet to be uncovered. Is this city Ubar? Unless written evidence is found, perhaps in the form of carved inscriptions, absolute confirmation may be impossible, but many archaeologists believe that the city uncovered by Clapp and Hedges is indeed Ubar. Whatever its name, the site is the oldest known settlement in southern Arabia. The excavators have found Roman, Greek, and Syrian artifacts, goods acquired through trade. Some of the Syrian artifacts are 4,000 years old.

Ubar was said to have been wiped out in a sudden cataclysm, and the Ash Shisar site did vanish suddenly, destroyed by the very thing that gave it life: a 40-foot-deep limestone cavern beneath the desert's surface. The cavern held water and was the source of the city's wells and of the water that irrigated Ubar's famed orchards. One day—probably between the 4th and the 6th century A.D., although

A radar image of the area around Ubar, taken from a satellite. The white band across the center is a *wadi,* the dry bed of a stream. Ubar was located near the *wadi,* close to the center of this picture. The fainter tracks that converge on the center are the ancient caravan trails that led to Ubar.

the date may never be known for certain—the roof of this cavern collapsed. The city sank into the cavern and was soon covered by drifting sands, forgotten until ancient geography, travelers' tales, and space-age technology were brought together to reveal its location.

It will be years, decades even, before archaeologists have learned what the ruins of Ubar can tell us about life and commerce in ancient Arabia. But already the site has caused scholars to rewrite a page of history. It is proof that a complex and sophisticated civilization existed in southern Arabia centuries earlier than archaeologists had previously thought. Like other lost cities that have been unearthed by explorers and archaeologists, Ubar has widened our window into the past.

The discovery of "lost cities" appeals to our love of excitement and our thirst for knowledge. The explorers and scientists who found and excavated ancient cities were adventurers. Sometimes their discoveries came after long and patient searching, as when Heinrich Schliemann unearthed the ruins of Troy. Sometimes discoveries happened suddenly and surprisingly, as when U.S. Army officer James Hervey Simpson stumbled upon the cliff dwellings of a lost people in the American Southwest. Either way, such discoveries were first-class stories. They make fascinating reading for armchair adventurers today.

Yet the discovery of a lost city is only the beginning of its story. Once discovered, each site must be investigated and studied before it yields up its secrets. An ancient city may hold clues to ancient religions, the origins of cultures, and patterns of trade and warfare among our ancestors, but these clues are not always easy to piece together. The study of a rediscovered city is an adventure in itself, requiring years of painstaking research and reassessment. Sometimes the discoverer's own ideas are later found to be incorrect, as was the case with Great Zimbabwe in Africa and Machu Picchu in South America.

Methods in archaeology have changed since the days of Johann Burckhardt and Charles Texier, when explorers and antiquarians poked around in remote corners of the world, looking for interesting ruins to describe to the folks back home. Some of the early explorers of ancient cities were little more than enthusiastic treasure hunters, burrowing frantically in all directions in the hope of

uncovering spectacular finds. Today's explorers are meticulous scientists who measure and photograph every bit of broken pottery, believing that the humble relics of everyday life can reveal as much about a bygone civilization as its grandest monuments.

Building upon the work of those who have gone before, each generation of scholars adds something new to our knowledge of ancient cities and the civilizations they represent. Copán and other Maya sites in Mexico and Central America, for example, have been studied for a century and a half, yet the 1990s have produced important new insights into Maya culture and history. New discoveries are still being made in the field—in 1992 a graduate student from the University of Pennsylvania unearthed a buried royal tomb in Copán. And new lost cities are still being discovered. In late 1995 an international team of archaeologists announced that they had located Urkesh, the long-lost capital of an ancient people called the Hurrians, in northwestern Syria. The Hurrians flourished 4,000 years ago, but the location of their capital was lost after their kingdom fell into decline. Less than one percent of the newly found site has been mapped and excavated; archaeologists expect to make many remarkable discoveries there in the years ahead.

As the discoverers of Ubar and Urkesh have reminded us, the great age of archaeology is far from over. Lucky travelers and hardworking scientists are still unlocking the keys to the past. Who knows how many more lost cities are out there waiting to be found?

Recent archaeological work at Petra. Although Petra was one of the first ancient cities to be explored in modern times, the site continues to yield new discoveries and new knowledge.

Chronology

before 4000 B.C.
Ur established in Sumer (modern Iraq)

3300 B.C.
Sumerians have developed writing

3000 B.C.
Settlement established at Troy (present-day Turkey)

2500 B.C.
Nineveh is important Sumerian city

2300 B.C.
Ur reaches peak of importance

around 2000 B.C.
Settlement begins at Ubar in Arabian Peninsula

1900–1470 B.C.
Minoan civilization of Crete reaches its height

around 1700 B.C.
Hattusha (near modern Boghazkeui, Turkey) becomes Hittite capital

13th century B.C.
Era of Trojan history celebrated in Homer's *Iliad*

1200 B.C.
Hattusha destroyed in downfall of Hittite empire

8th century B.C.
Iliad is composed

6th century B.C.
Nabataeans begin building Petra (present-day Jordan)

around 400 B.C.
Ur abandoned

around 250 B.C.
Maya begin building Copán (present-day Honduras)

A.D. 106
Petra becomes part of Roman Empire

200
Anasazi culture begins to form in American Southwest

4th–6th century
Ubar is destroyed

6th century
Petra declines; location of Troy is lost

7th–9th century
Peak of Maya settlement at Copán

9th century
Khmer rulers begin building Angkor (present-day Cambodia)

10th–11th century
Permanent settlement of Great Zimbabwe (present-day Zimbabwe) begins

1200
Inca culture develops in the Andes Mountains

1250
Great Zimbabwe reaches peak of its importance as a trade center

11th–13th century
High point of Anasazi civilization

12th century
Angkor Wat built

1431

Khmers abandon Angkor

1438

Pachacuti founds the Inca empire

16th century

Great Zimbabwe is abandoned

1532

Pizarro's conquistadors invade Peru

1572

Last Inca emperor is killed

1812

Johann Ludwig Burckhardt visits Petra and records its location

1820

Claudius Rich begins looking for Nineveh at Kuyunjik, Iraq

1834

Charles Texier finds ruins of Hattusha

1839

John Lloyd Stephens and Frederick Catherwood rediscover Copán and begin Maya studies

1845–50

Austen Henry Layard excavates Nimrud and Nineveh in Iraq

1849

James Hervey Simpson reports on Anasazi sites at Canyon de Chelly and Chaco Canyon

1860

Henri Mouhot visits Angkor and describes it for the world

1870

Heinrich Schliemann begins excavating the ruins of Troy in Hissarlik, Turkey

1871

Karl Mauch finds ruins of Great Zimbabwe

1873

Schliemann finds "Priam's treasure"

1900

Arthur Evans begins excavating the palace of Knossos in Crete

1901

Harriet Boyd excavates Minoan town of Gournia

1906

Hugo Winckler begins excavations at Bogazköy

1911

Hiram Bingham finds Inca ruins at Machu Picchu and Vilcabamba

1922

Leonard Woolley begins excavating Sumerian city of Ur

1929

Gertrude Caton-Thompson establishes African origin of Great Zimbabwe

1989–92

Royal tombs discovered at Copán

1990

Archaeologists discover a 6th-century Christian church in Petra

1991

Scientists uncover buried ruins of Ubar

1993

Representatives from 30 nations meet to discuss saving Angkor

1995

Archaeologists locate Urkesh, lost Hurrian capital, in Syria

Further Reading

Ancient Cities and Civilizations in General

Bacon, Edward. *The Great Archaeologists.* Indianapolis, Ind.: Bobbs-Merrill, 1976.

Ceram, C. W. *Gods, Graves, and Scholars.* New York: Bantam, 1976.

Daniel, Glyn. *A Hundred and Fifty Years of Archaeology.* Revised edition. Cambridge, Mass.: Harvard University Press, 1976.

———. *A Short History of Archaeology.* London: Thames and Hudson, 1981.

de Camp, L. Sprague, and Catherine de Camp. *Citadels of Mystery.* 5th ed. New York: Ballantine, 1973.

Fagan, Brian M. *The Adventure of Archaeology.* Washington, D.C.: National Geographic Society, 1985.

———. *Eyewitness to Discovery.* New York: Oxford University Press, 1997.

———. *In the Beginning.* Boston: Little, Brown, 1985.

———, ed. *The Oxford Companion to Archaeology.* New York: Oxford University Press.

———. *Quest for the Past: Great Discoveries in Archaeology.* Reading, Mass.: Addison-Wesley, 1978.

———. *Time Detectives: How Archeologists Use Technology to Recapture the Past.* New York: Simon and Schuster, 1995.

Hawkes, Jacquetta. *The Atlas of Ancient Archaeology.* New York: McGraw-Hill, 1974.

Picard, Jean-Charles. *Larousse Encyclopedia of Archaeology.* New York: Larousse, 1983.

Robbins, Lawrence H. *Stones, Bones, and Ancient Cities.* New York: St. Martin's, 1990.

Sherratt, Andrew. *The Cambridge Encyclopedia of Archaeology.* New York: Cambridge University Press, 1980.

Ward, Anne. *Adventures in Archaeology.* New York: Larousse, 1977.

Whitehouse, Ruth. *The Facts on File Dictionary of Archaeology.* New York: Facts on File, 1983.

Willey, Gordon R., and Jeremy A. Sabloff. *A History of American Archaeology.* San Francisco: W. H. Freeman, 1980.

Egyptology

Aldred, Cyril. *The Egyptians.* London: Thames and Hudson, 1984.

Clayton, Peter. *The Rediscovery of Ancient Egypt.* New York: Portland House, 1990

Fagan, Brian. *The Rape of the Nile.* New York: Charles Scribner's Sons, 1975.

Greener, Leslie. *The Discovery of Egypt.* New York: Viking, 1966.

Hoving, Thomas. *Tutankhamun: The Untold Story.* New York: Simon and Schuster, 1978.

National Geographic Society. *Ancient Eygpt.* Washington, D.C.: National Geographic Society, 1978.

Reeves, Nicholas. *The Complete Tutankhamun.* London: Thames and Hudson, 1990.

Time-Life Books. *Egypt: Land of the Pharaohs.* Alexandria, Va.: Time-Life Books, 1992.

Petra

Browning, Iain. *Petra.* Revised Edition. London: Chatto and Windus, 1982.

Diamond, Jared. "Pack Rat Historians." *Natural History,* February 1991.

Glueck, Nelson. *Deities and Dolphins: The Story of the Nabataeans.* New York: Farrar, Straus and Giroux, 1965.

Hedges, Chris. "Ancient City of Petra Is Yielding Its Secrets." *New York Times,* 4 January 1994.

Hills, Ann. "Saving the Rose-Red City." *History Today,* February 1993.

Nineveh and the Assyrians

Fagan, Brian. *Return to Babylon: Travelers, Archaeologists, and Monuments in Mesopotamia.* Boston: Little, Brown, 1979.

Finegan, Jack. *Archaeological History of the Ancient Middle East.* New York: Dorset, 1979.

Lloyd, Seton. *Foundations in the Dust: The Story of Mesopotamian Exploration.* New York: Thames and Hudson, 1980.

Roux, Georges. *Ancient Iraq*. London: Penguin, 1992.

Saggs, H. W. F. *The Might That Was Assyria*. New York: St. Martin's, 1984.

Time-Life Books. *Mesopotamia: The Mighty Kings*. Alexandria, Va.: Time-Life Books, 1995.

Waterfield, Gordon. *Layard of Nineveh*. New York: Frederick A. Praeger, 1963.

Hattusha and the Hittites

Bittel, Kurt. *Hattusha: The Capital of the Hittites*. New York: Oxford University Press, 1970.

Ceram, C. W. *The Secret of the Hittites: The Discovery of an Ancient Empire*. Translated by Richard and Clara Winston. New York: Knopf, 1956.

Gurney, O. R. *The Hittites*. New York: Penguin, 1991.

Lehmann, Johannes. *The Hittites: People of a Thousand Gods*. Translated by J. Maxwell Brownjohn. New York: Viking, 1977.

Time-Life Books. *Anatolia: Cauldron of Cultures*. Alexandria, Va.: Time-Life Books, 1995.

Copán and the Maya

Brunhouse, Robert L. *In Search of the Maya: The First Archaeologists*. New York: Ballantine, 1973.

Coe, Michael D. *The Maya*. 4th ed. New York: Thames and Hudson, 1991.

———. *Breaking the Maya Code*. New York: Thames and Hudson, 1992.

Fagan, Brian M. *Kingdoms of Gold, Kingdoms of Jade: The Americas before Columbus*. London: Thames and Hudson, 1991.

Fash, William L., Jr., and Barbara Fash. "Maya Resurrection." *Natural History*, April 1996.

———. "Scribes, Warriors, and Kings: The Lives of the Copán Maya." *Archaeology*, May–June 1990.

Fasquelle, Ricardo Agurcia, and William L. Fash, Jr. "Copán: A Royal Tomb Discovered." *National Geographic*, October 1989.

———. "Maya Artistry Unearthed." *National Geographic*, September 1991.

Gallenkamp, Charles. *Maya: The Riddle and Rediscovery of a Lost Civilization*. 3rd rev. ed. New York: Viking, 1985.

Hammond, Norman. *Ancient Maya Civilization*. New Brunswick, N.J.: Rutgers University Press, 1982.

———. "Unearthing the Oldest Known Maya." *National Geographic*, July 1982.

Lemonick, Michael D., and Guy Garcia. "Secrets of the Maya." *Time*, 9 August 1993.

Sabloff, Jeremy A. *The New Archaeology and the Ancient Maya*. New York: Scientific American Books, 1990.

———. "The Maya Rediscovered." *Natural History*, January 1991.

Schele, Linda, and David Freidal. *A Forest of Kings*. New York: William Morrow, 1990.

Sharer, Robert J., and Elin Dannien, eds. *New Theories on the Ancient Maya*. Philadelphia: University Museum, University of Pennsylvania, 1992.

Stephens, John Lloyd. *Incidents of Travel in Central American, Chiapas, and Yucatan*. 2 vols. 1841. Reprint, New York: Dover, 1969.

———. *Incidents of Travel in Yucatan*. 2 vols. 1843. Reprint, New York: Dover, 1963.

Stuart, George. "Copán: City of Kings and Commoners." *National Geographic*, October 1989.

Time-Life Books. *The Magnificent Maya*. Alexandria, Va.: Time-Life Books, 1993.

Von Hagen, Victor W. *Search for the Maya: The Story of Stephens and Catherwood*. Revised edition. London: Gordon and Cremonesi, 1978.

Chaco Canyon and the Anasazi

Ambler, J. Richard. *The Anasazi*. Flagstaff: Museum of Northern Arizona Press, 1989.

Anderson, Douglas, and Barbara Anderson. *Chaco Canyon*. Tucson: Southwest Parks and Monuments Association, 1981.

Brody, J. J. *The Anasazi*. New York: Rizzoli, 1990.

Canby, Thomas Y. "The Anasazi." *National Geographic*, November 1982.

Ferguson, William, and Arthur Rohn. *Anasazi Ruins of the Southwest in Color*. Albuquerque: University of New Mexico Press, 1990.

Frazier, Kendrick. *People of Chaco.* New York: Norton, 1986.

Lekson, Stephen H. *Great Pueblo Architecture of Chaco Canyon, New Mexico.* Albuquerque: University of New Mexico Press, 1989.

Lister, Robert H., and Florence Lister. *Archaeology and Archaeologists: Chaco Canyon.* Albuquerque: University of New Mexico Press, 1981.

McNitt, Frank. *Richard Wetherill: Anasazi.* Albuquerque: University of New Mexico Press, 1966.

Roberts, David. "The Old Ones of the Southwest." *National Geographic*, April 1996.

Stuart, Gene S. *America's Ancient Cities.* Washington, D.C.: National Geographic Society, 1989.

Time-Life Books. *Mound Builders and Cliff Dwellers.* Alexandria, Va.: Time-Life Books, 1992.

Wicklein, John. "Spirit Paths of the Anasazi." *Archaeology*, January–February 1994.

Angkor and the Khmers

Brownmiller, Susan. "At Last, Angkor Wat." *Travel and Leisure*, October 1992.

Ciochon, Russell. "Jungle Monuments of Angkor." *Natural History*, January 1990.

Ciochon, Russell, and Jamie James. "The Glory That Was Angkor." *Archaeology*, March–April 1994.

Coedes, George. *Angkor, An Introduction.* Translated by Emily Floyd Gardiner. New York: Oxford University Press, 1970.

Cohen, Joan L. *Angkor: Monuments of the God-Kings.* New York: Abrams, 1973.

Freeman, Michael, and Roger Warner. *Angkor: The Hidden Glories.* Boston: Houghton Mifflin, 1990.

Hornik, Richard. "The Battle of Angkor." *Time*, 6 April 1992.

Macdonald, M. *Angkor and the Khmers.* New York: Oxford University Press, 1987.

Mouhot, Henri. *Travels in Siam, Cambodia, and Laos, 1858–1860.* 1863. Reprint, New York: Oxford University Press, 1989. Introduction by Michael Smithies.

Rooney, Dawn. *Angkor: Temples of Cambodia's Kings.* Tulsa, Okla.: NTC, 1993.

Time-Life Books. *Southeast Asia: A Past Regained.* Alexandria, Va.: Time-Life Books, 1995.

White, Peter T. "The Temples of Angkor." *National Geographic*, May 1982.

Troy

Brackman, A. C. *The Dream of Troy.* New York: Van Nostrand Reinhold, 1974.

Deuel, Leo, ed. *Memoirs of Heinrich Schliemann.* New York: Harper and Row, 1977.

Fleischman, John. "Digging Deeper into the Mysteries of Troy." *Smithsonian*, January 1992.

Mellink, Machteld J., ed. *Troy and the Trojan War.* Bryn Mawr, Pa.: Bryn Mawr College, 1986.

Meyer, Karl E. "The Hunt for Priam's Treasure." *Archaeology*, November–December 1993.

Ottaway, James H. "New Assault on Troy." *Arachaeology*, September–October 1991.

Rose, Mark. "What Did Schliemann Find?" *Archaeology*, November–December 1993.

Schliemann, Heinrich. *Troy and Its Remains.* 1875. Reprint, New York: Benjamin Blom, 1968.

Time-Life Books. *Wondrous Realms of the Aegean.* Alexandria, Va.: Time-Life Books, 1993.

Traill, David A. *Schliemann of Troy: Treasure and Deceit.* New York: St. Martin's, 1996.

Wood, Michael. *In Search of the Trojan War.* New York: Facts On File, 1985.

Great Zimbabwe

Beach, D. N. *The Shona and Zimbabwe, 900–1850.* New York: Africana Publishing, 1980.

Burke, E. E., ed. *The Journals of Carl Mauch.* Translated by F. O. Bernhard. Salisbury: National Archives of Rhodesia, 1969.

Connah, Graham. *African Civilizations.* Cambridge: Cambridge University Press, 1987.

Davidson, Basil. *The Lost Cities of Africa.* Boston: Little, Brown, 1987.

Garlake, Peter. *Great Zimbabwe.* London: Thames and Hudson, 1973.

———. *Life at Great Zimbabwe.* Zimbabwe: Mambo Press, 1983.

Huffman, Thomas N. *A Guide to the Great Zimbabwe Ruins.* Salisbury: Trustees of the National Museums and Monuments of Rhodesia, 1976.

———. *Symbols in Stone: Unravelling the Mystery of Great Zimbabwe.* Johannesburg, South Africa: Witwatersrand University Press, 1987.

Mallows, Wilfrid. *The Mystery of the Great Zimbabwe: A New Solution*. New York: Norton, 1984.

Time-Life Books. *Africa's Glorious Legacy*. Alexandria, Va.: Time-Life Books, 1994.

Knossos, Gournia, and the Minoans

Allsebrook, Mary. *Born to Rebel: The Life of Harriet Boyd Hawes*. Oxford: Oxbow Books, 1992.

Castelden, Rodney, *The Knossos Labyrinth*. London: Routledge, 1990.

Cottrell, Leonard. *The Bull of Minos: The Discoveries of Schliemann and Evans*. New York: Facts on File, 1984.

Evans, Arthur. *The Palace of Minos at Knossos*. London: Macmillan, 1930.

Evans, Joan. *Time and Chance: The Story of Arthur Evans and His Forebears*. 1943. Reprint, Westport, Conn.: Greenwood, 1974.

Graham, J. Walter. *The Palaces of Crete*. Revised edition. Princeton, N.J.: Princeton University Press, 1987.

Hood, Sinclair. *The Minoans: The Story of Bronze Age Crete*. New York: Praeger, 1971.

Platon, Nicholas. *Zakros: The Discovery of a Lost Palace of Ancient Crete*. London: Thames and Hudson, 1969.

Sakellarakis, Jannis, and Efi Sapouna-Sakellarakis. "Drama of Death in a Minoan Temple." *National Geographic*, February 1981.

Time-Life Books. *Wondrous Realms of the Aegean*. Alexandria, Va.: Time-Life Books, 1993.

Warren, Peter. *The Aegean Civilizations*. New York: Peter Bedrick, 1989.

————. "Knossos: New Excavations and Discoveries." *Archaeology*, July–August, 1984.

Machu Picchu and the Incas

Barnard, Charles N. "Machu Picchu: City in the Sky." *National Geographic Traveler*, January–February 1993.

Bingham, Alfred. *Portrait of an Explorer: Hiram Bingham, Discoverer of Machu Picchu*. Ames: Iowa State University Press, 1989.

Bingham, Hiram. *Lost City of the Incas*. 1948. Reprint, New York: Atheneum, 1971.

Hemming, John. *Machu Picchu*. New York: Newsweek Books, 1981.

Kendall, Ann. *Everyday Life of the Incas*. New York: Dorset, 1973.

McIntyre, Loren. *The Incredible Incas and Their Timeless Land*. Washington, D.C.: National Geographic Society, 1975.

————. "Lost Empire of the Incas." *National Geographic*, December 1973.

Time-Life Books. *Incas: Lords of Gold and Glory*. Alexandria, Va.: Time-Life Books, 1992.

Ur and the Sumerians

Baumann, Hans. *The Land of Ur*. Translated by Stella Humphries. New York: Oxford University Press, 1969.

Crawford, Harriet. *Sumer and the Sumerians*. Cambridge, England: Cambridge University Press, 1991.

Fagan, Brian M. *Return to Babylon: Travelers, Archaeologists, and Monuments in Mesopotamia*. Boston: Little, Brown, 1979.

Finegan, Jack. *Archaeological History of the Ancient Middle East*. New York: Dorset, 1979.

Glubok, Shirley, ed. *Discovering the Royal Tombs at Ur*. London: Collier-Macmillan, 1969.

Hamblin, Dora-Jane, and the editors of Time-Life Books. *The First Cities*. New York: Time-Life Books, 1973.

Kramer, Samuel Noah. *History Begins at Sumer*. Philadelphia: University of Pennsylvania Press, 1981.

Reade, Julian. *Mesopotamia*. London: British Museum Press, 1991.

Severy, Merle. "Iraq: Crucible of Civilization." *National Geographic*, May 1991.

Wenke, Robert J. *Patterns in Prehistory*. New York: Oxford University Press, 1990.

Winstone, H. V. F. *Woolley of Ur: The Life of Sir Leonard Woolley*. London: Secker and Warburg, 1990.

Woolley, C. Leonard. *Ur "of the Chaldees."* 1929. Reprint, Ithaca, N.Y.: Cornell University Press, 1982.

Ubar

Crabb, Charlane. "Ancient Center of Frankincense Trade Uncovered." *Discover*, January 1993.

Fiennes, Ranulph. *The Atlantis of the Sands: The Search for the Lost City of Ubar*. London: Bloomsbury, 1992.

Ostling, Richard N. "Arabia's Lost Sand Castle." *Time*, 17 February 1992.

Wilford, John Noble. "On the Trail from the Sky: Roads Point to a Lost City." *New York Times*, 5 February 1992.

Index

Picture Credits

*R*ebecca Stefoff has written more than 50 books for young adults, specializing in geography and biography. Her lifelong interest in reading and collecting travel narratives is reflected in such titles as *Lewis and Clark, Magellan and the Discovery of the World Ocean, Marco Polo and the Medieval Travelers, Vasco da Gama and the Portuguese Explorers, The Viking Explorers,* and numerous books on China, Japan, Mongolia, the Middle East, and Latin America. Her books on exploration include *Accidental Explorers, Women of the World,* and *Scientific Explorers.* Ms. Stefoff has served as editorial director of two Chelsea House series, *Places and Peoples of the World* and *Let's Discover Canada,* and as a geography consultant for the *Silver Burdett Countries* series. She earned her Ph.D. at the University of Pennsylvania and lives in Portland, Oregon.